Collected Poems and Plays

WYNDHAM LEWIS

Collected Poems and Plays

edited by ALAN MUNTON

with an introduction by C.H.SISSON

Carcanet•Manchester

SBN 85635-371-X

First published in 1979
by Carcanet Press.
For information, contact the publisher.
Carcanet New Press Ltd.
330 Corn Exchange
Manchester, M4 3BG

Printed in the United States of America

CONTENTS

ILLUSTRATIONS

ACKNOWLEDGEMENTS

MY first thanks are due to Mrs Anne Wyndham Lewis for allowing the material in this edition to be published and for her interest in the project.

For access to manuscripts, I wish to thank the Librarian and staff of the Rare Book Room, Olin Library, Cornell University, and particularly Mrs Joan Winterkorn, who pointed out to me certain items I should not otherwise have seen; and the Poetry Collection of the Lockwood Memorial Library, State University of New York at Buffalo.

I have had a great deal of help from Lewis's former publishers, and would like to thank Lord Harmsworth of Egham (Desmond Harmsworth); Mr Peter du Sautoy and Faber and Faber Ltd; and Associated Book Publishers Ltd. For photographs of drawings and paintings I wish to thank Pier van der Kruk of Utrecht; Walter Michel; Catharine Waley of the Courtauld Institute of Art; and Gordon Shaw of the Cambridgeshire College of Arts and Technology, Cambridge. Omar Pound, Philip Grover and Bernard Lafourcade have been extremely helpful with bibliographical materials, and I have received help on particular points from Edgell Rickword, C. H. Sisson, Paul Edwards and C. J. Fox.

ALAN MUNTON

The second edition of this collection has given me the opportunity to make a number of minor corrections to the text, as well as to a more obvious error on page 37. I am particularly grateful to Frank Fitzpatrick who, without announcing his intention, very kindly provided me with a list of almost all these corrections.

A.M.
March, 1981

INTRODUCTION

WHEN Alan Munton was starting work on this edition of Lewis's *Poems and Plays* he took me back to the rooms he and his wife were then occupying in Cambridge to hear a recording of *One-Way Song*. An unexpected voice filled the room. These verses, with more than their share of exclamation marks, rhetorical question marks, and brazen assertions of one sort and another, were read by Lewis in tones which were gentle, explanatory, elucidatory, as of some rather upper-class professor —of course of a generation before any of those at present holding professorial chairs. The verses themselves had been familiar to me since the thirties when they were first published, but Lewis's reading cast a new light on them, exactly as a reading by Yeats or Eliot affects one's apprehension of what they were about in their poems. *One-Way Song* belongs to that most unexpected of categories—in the twentieth century—the didactic poem; and because Lewis was a writer of genius he managed to give this disused form not the smell of dust from the past but the breath and, it must be admitted, some of the rattle of the contemporary world.

Lewis was—and it was not the least of his many gifts—a popularizer, though he somehow never managed to reach the great publics he felt qualified to teach. In one of his many characterizations of himself he says:

> I am rather what Mr Shaw would have been like if he had been an artist—I here use 'artist' in the widest possible sense—if he had not been an Irishman, if he had been a young man when the Great War occurred, if he had studied painting and philosophy instead of economics and Ibsen, and if he had been more richly endowed with imagination, emotion, intellect and a few other things.

Blasting and Bombardiering, 1937, p. 3.

To show he was being modest in comparison with the wide-mouthed Irishman Lewis added that Shaw 'said he was a finer fellow than Shakespeare. I merely prefer myself to Mr Shaw.' I suppose to the middle-aged, middle-brow public of the thirties this must have seemed an outrageous claim, but time has changed all that. Shaw has fallen from intellectual view so completely that quite dull people might now entertain, unappalled, the possibility that Lewis might have had the better brain of the two.

There is, in fact, something of Shaw's chaotic method of attack in the endless little pseudo-aggressions, the ironies, and the discursive flightiness of Lewis's popularizing style. If Lewis was less successful, it is partly that what he was attacking was so much more resistant. The liberal conscience into which Shaw shot his arrows was asking to be made to wince; the pleasure of being scandalous was easy to come by, in Shaw's day. The great politicized masses of the rich and not-so-rich who were Lewis's targets could hardly be made to stir in their dogmatic slumbers. They loved their prejudices too much. Moreover, Lewis had mapped out this great field of obtuseness before people had realized, even dimly, that they were in it. And for being before one's time in any field the contemporary penalties are always heavy.

There must be many who are acquainted with some of Lewis's brilliant array of work—his paintings and drawings, his fiction from *The Wild Body* to *The Human Age*, or his critical and theoretical works such as *Men Without Art* and *Time and Western Man*—who have not yet been introduced to the poems and plays—plays which are not exactly plays and poems which do not answer to what most people expect under that designation. These readers will find in this volume a new handling of some of Lewis's characteristic themes—which take on a fresh meaning with, for example, the figures of Hanp and Arghol— limp, unwieldy titans with a touch of the stage property about them, against their background of 'RED OF TARNISHED COPPER PREDOMINANT COLOUR, UP-ENDED EGG-BOXES, CASKS, RUBBLE, CHEVAUX DE FRISE, COLLECTIONS OF CLAY-LOAM AND BRICK-DUST', and so on. Their dialogue, in true Lewis style, oscillates between philosophic matter on which the essay-appendix, *The Physics of the Not-Self*, also here reprinted, offers a commentary, and the homeliest social comedy, as in

HANP (*growling in his corner*): We can't all be gentlemen. We can't all be fine gentlemen!
ARGHOL (*in a dull roar of surprise*): Why should we wish to be that in God's name, I don't understand you, Hanp!
HANP: No nor yet vegetarians—turning up our noses at lamb.
ARGHOL (*mournfully*): Why vegetarian? The vegetarian is no gentleman.
HANP: No? I didn't know. I thought he was for sure.

ARGHOL: Certainly not. There you are quite wrong.

HANP: Go on! Isn't he one? I made sure he was.

ARGHOL: By ·no means. Decidedly not. Gentleman and
vegetarian should never be mentioned in the same breath.

Two versions of *Enemy of the Stars* are given—from 1914 and
1932 respectively—as well as the text of the even less-known
The Ideal Giant, reprinted from *The Little Review* of May, 1918.

It is to the poems that the reader who does not know Lewis's
work already may be advised to turn first, for they may be
approached by anyone with any acquaintance with twentieth-
century English poetry, simply as work with a tone and manner
not to be found elsewhere in that literature. *One-Way Song* is
an exhilarating read, in a forceful and familiar style which has
some affinities with Kipling's, although accent and subject-
matter are remote indeed from those of the great balladist. Of
course Lewis is nowhere near to being the technical master
that Kipling was, in the matter of verse. In this field he is a
dashing and magnificent amateur—and in verse successful
amateurism is rare indeed. Lewis brought to this flight from
his ordinary modes of expression an immense gift of language,
a vein of satire unequalled in English in this century or the
last, and a pressure of subject-matter which wells from the
deepest sources of his art.

This volume contains, besides *One-Way Song*, the text of an
early poem, 'Grignolles', which was published in 1910. The
poem is far from having on it the full stamp of the mature Lewis,
but looking back on it we can see that it is as if a powerful mind
and an unclouded eye had irrupted into the field of Georgian
country-poetry, had seized upon it and made it something of
its own. The piece is remarkable in its own right for a certain
invincible solidity. Alan Munton has also turned up one or two
unpublished poems and fragments, which are given in an appen-
dix. He has, I think rightly, omitted the wad of early sonnets,
some lines of which Lewis claimed to confuse with Shakespeare's. These were a youthful error of Lewis's time at the
Slade. It would add nothing to the understanding of Lewis's
work to publish these mercifully unprinted early texts, which
are of interest mainly as showing how blindly even a literary
genius may grope in his early years, under the weight of youthful emotions. The crude faculty of imitation may well be most
overwhelming in someone for whom words are to be a great

resource. One example, chosen among the sonnets with such titles as 'Lust', 'To the Spirit of Poetry', 'Barren Hours' and 'Solitude', may serve for all:

>   A wealth of soul of which she hath not ease
> Hath woman,—as a treasure leagued by fate,
> A trust that, if unclaim'd, disconsolate
> And full of swift alarms and maladies
> Her life doth leave; if on this wealth she seize
> Or squander aught, some conscience strange doth rate
> The expense, though with her wealth commensurate,—
> And all she spends seems stolen and nought hers.
>
> Too great a soul hath woman, too great scope:
> Yet ne'er with franchise doth her wealth employ,—
> Or in some menial manner,—some poor hope
> Doth gild, or stints some nobler with alloy;
> And man doth oft some dark despoiler deem,
> So basely lavish, she that buys his dream.

The satirist had not yet been born, the blind energy had not yet begun to find a verbal outlet. The leap from such work to 'Grignolles' is immense. In the latter poem the words already answer, if still a little stiffly, to the perception. In *One-Way Song* there is no matter in the author's repertoire of theory and satire which cannot be handled. Lewis's technical mastery is never enough for him to exhaust himself in a poem or a line—which is hardly surprising, considering how many other masteries he possessed. Though he sometimes uses fourteeners to rousing effect, his most characteristic medium is the heroic couplet. He managed the feat, which was quite extraordinary, and in the thirties extraordinarily difficult, of using that form in a manner which is entirely personal and does not recall the dead tradition of the eighteenth century to which Roy Campbell fell victim and from which even Edgell Rickword was not absolutely free. This is, perhaps, partly because Lewis was so possessed by his subject-matter that it entirely determined his manner. There is perhaps a subtler reason. It is that Lewis, in writing 'like Boileau', as he not altogether plausibly said, felt not the least inclination to pretend to the moral certainties of another age; it is those certainties which are really the backbone of classical satire. Lewis himself claimed that 'the greatest satire is non-moral'. If there is a general difficulty about

One-Way Song, it is because there is not one plain satiric view-point but as it were a dramatic proliferation of characters speaking one beside the other and leaving the reader in suspense.

This book can be read for pure pleasure by anyone who is not put off by a vigour rare in the literature of this century. Alan Munton has added notes which will be invaluable to those who seek to set these extraordinary productions against the wider background of Lewis's work as a whole.

C. H. SISSON
August 1978

GRIGNOLLES
(*Brittany*)

Grignolles is a town grown bald
with age; its blue naked crown
of houses is barer than any hill,
on its small hill;—it is a grey town.

It is like a cathedral, crowding and still,
all of a piece, like one sheer house;
like a town built for worship, and called
Grignolles, from the land thereabout.

But it is like a cathedral from which have decayed
all after-thoughts and generous things
added—the warm gradual weft—
all down-coverings from its naked wings.

It seems only first buildings are left,
the virgin soul of first architects;
only the first dream of a town as it leapt
in the brains of the lonely peasants—projects

which the dim granges shaped from their sides,
and a wilderness of gaunt fields that
needed a house as each holding does—
but a great warm house more human than that.

Now something of that first savageness,
and the keen sadness of first plains,
(although the country's grown bourgeois and green)
to the town has come as its soul wanes.

Within, Grignolles is listless and sweet;
its veiled life is not conscious how
its wandering cairn of walls can suggest
in one wild whole things dead now:

just as a man forgets Time's waste,
and his soul's crumbling, and is blind
to a grandeur a little distance gives it—
lives a life veiled, moody and kind.

In the town people live an insect life,
there are three sorts of house in its streets,
and many gardens hid in its walls;
there are two sorts of people one meets.

Its gardens are odorous wells each house
hides with high walls—you never see
these—but you know each bleak great house
has its harem—hid flowers and wind-scented tree.

Of the two sorts of people there met,
one are old—a fierce shy race,
an old life revived as their soul dried;
the others are young, with bold mild face.

Its bare houses are stuccoed and wide.
Grey like the stone-grey of the sky.
Blue like the dull shade of stone when wet:
and white, to tell its small inns by,

as over the porch hangs mistletoe.
Its houses are bleak windy fronts
with stormy windows; or cabins low;
and wandering convents, and sheds chapels once.

One-Way Song

WYNDHAM LEWIS

With a foreword by T. S. Eliot

BY WYNDHAM LEWIS

ENGINE FIGHT-TALK

THE SONG OF
THE MILITANT ROMANCE

IF SO THE MAN YOU
ARE

ONE-WAY SONG

ENVOI

LONDON
FABER AND FABER LIMITED
24 RUSSELL SQUARE

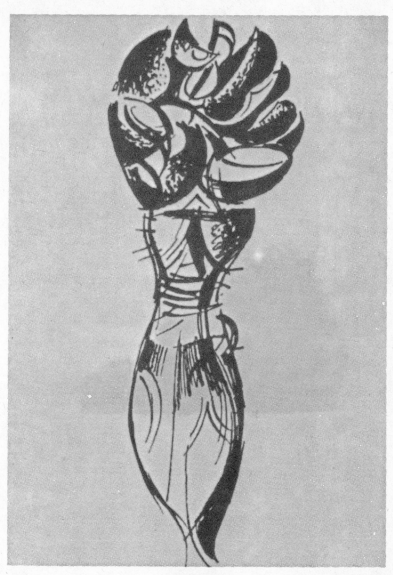

**ENGINE
FIGHT-TALK**

ENGINE FIGHT-TALK

I said (and I always say these things with the same voice)
'Say it with locomotives! Mark well that animal puff!'
Each man-jack of them marked it, every man-jack—all were
      boys.
'If you must, say it with locofocos! Radical Tammany stuff!
Hot and heavy! As if you meant it! Don't stick at a rough
      house—real rough!'

But at 'radical', magical vocable, claps crashed forth of stunning
      applause,
Though rattle-proof, that straightway shattered my heavily
      pillared doors!

'Say it' said I 'with half-machines!' And then, sublimely hoarse
With horrid pleasure they *said* it, with puff-puffs—roars upon
      roars.
The place was soon congested as with a fog of escaping steam.
I gazed in through it at the team-work proudly, of my loud
      responsive team.

'Well that's enough' at last I said. 'You've put your backs into
      that all right.
You said it with locomotives honies! That will do I guess for
      tonight.'

And I sketched them the Flying Scot—proudest and bravest
      of trains—
In bold chalk outlines bodily, with black alphabet of smoke.
And I drew beside it the World, with grey chalk for where it
      rains,
And for where it's hottest, red. I looked up. Nobody spoke.

'Among machines, "the hearty"!' (I always explained things
      thus—
The human touch—makes wild cats kins). 'Not exactly *one of
      us*!
Still half a horse!' They saw it at once—not quite yet *it* of
      course.

'Instincts to graze, gallop, cavort!' They nodded. 'The full
      machine
Not yet—too close to flesh and blood—that's in fact really all
      I mean!'
They hurled their class-books at each other's heads, there were
      roars upon earsplitting roars.

'I said "Man's friend!"' with unction—duly I curled the lip.
'Overnight that eclipsed the horse—into a sad has-been
Threw down the camel—shipwrecked that "desert-ship"!
Put out of business all the craftsmen who grew fat on the
      classic scene.
In the motherland, shrivelled stooks and stubble. And as if
      that were not enough,
This novelty of compressed steam, did it not call the bluff
Of all the dark "Medicines" of those peoples under a god—
Nay with its puffing has it not got us all we have got!'

Tapping my mouth, in the same unbending tone,
I said (my voice is never raised the jot of a note above
The merest conversational half-drone),
'What comes out of our Backs now goes to stuff
Our Fronts—*as things are*.' And I took a pinch of snuff,
Just to make clear that habits that were Swift's
Were good enough for me. 'The smoke-screen lifts—
That put up by our natural conceit—
Showing us where we stand—if innocent of feet
We can be said to stand. Why yes it's somewhat rough
On you and me—Lord Byron, Pope, and Plato—
To find this life not worth even the proverbial potato!'

A stifled titter at this punctured the ponderous air
In the bodywork as it were (to be shoppy) of this most model
      class—
By me lately invented.—Slowly across my chest
I drew my strong serge walls, in the manner of bold Jack Tars.

'All in this bitch of an epoch is for Backness' again I said.
'Up *Backness* for countersign! Hark you, that identical voodoo
      stuff
Of Backness goes to compose even the marxist mahomet—

Of that false colossus—of all work and no circuses and bread.
Erected in contradiction to the cant of the cult of Love.
Up Cant of Reason—bow the knee! Long live the dogmatic
    dove!'

They found this a little difficult. 'False colossus' was very bad.
I could see them biting their fingernails behind the breastworks
    of their cribs.
I did not speak for a minute. I knew they must take for a cad
A man who was brutal to Marx, or at best to be regarded as
    mad.
So I had to win back their confidence. I did it with sundry fibs,
And looks of bursting conceit. At his ease at once each small
    lad
Rewreathed his smiles, asked to leave the room, or went back
    to his fish and chips.

Having stood two or three on the form, and having stood four
    or five in the corner
I took up my teaching again, avoiding the role of suborner.

I said (and I *never* make these remarks in aught but the
    haughtiest voice)
'Attend to all that begins with a busy smoke and noise;
There was never smoke where fire was not; no, I have never seen
A worth-while something begin in quiet.' The class was as keen
    as keen
To hear more of this—they tightened their ear drums. But I
    had other views.
So I turned up my notes on magic, engineering, Irish stews.

But poetry came out first. So I said in my usual tones
'Let us consider next how far the Past is our pigeon!
Should we *really* drive our ploughshare without compunction
    across its bones,
(If we have a ploughshare) or should we leave it (if we *can*) in
    its proper region?'
And every man-jack of my little chorus shouted,
Either *no* or *yes* or merely *oh*!—*no* byelaw of the classroom
    but was flouted.

I stood a dozen on the form, and told a dozen to stay behind,
Stuck six or eight in the corner—told the rest to jolly well
      mind!
I put birches in pickle publicly in view of the thunderstruck
      class.
I turned my back in a tantrum—but ambushed two more in
      the glass!

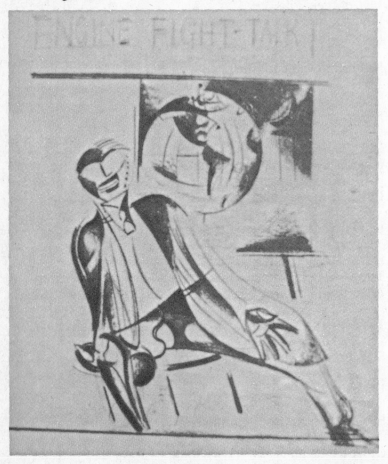

Schoolmaster (not previously published)

'I should like to know,' I said—the same voice as before—
'How it comes that Shakespeare caught the silhouette of Caesar.
I should like to know the reason why R. Browning's such a bore

In his doggerel novelettes, such a long-winded sort of geezer.
I should like to have you tell me why Browne's *Urn*
Makes all the Past with firework colours burn—
Why Taliesin steps in Peacock, I should be very glad to learn,
Or why the lungs of Guinevar swell with coarse breath again.

I would give my passport to find out what whore
Has come to live with Swinburne—I would fain
Find out what page the sorcerer John Keats tore
From the shut book—and how even Beckford came to wake
A litter of earthquaking spooks to make the walls of Lisbon shake.
Can you call up the consciousness that the sleepy Pater used
To wake the Middleages—with what senses was it fused?
For that matter explain to me how the pages of *Cathay*
Came out of the time-bound Ezra into the light of common day!'

Well all the boys were pleased. 'What is the volume, sir,
In Portuguese?' I smiled. This was young Percy Burke.
He put up a plea for synthesis: 'The Past's a jolly blur.
I like things sharp, like the light in Boston. I'm afraid that I
        demur.
Surely this rummaging in the medieval murk,
This pandering to the mighty vagueness of our hearts,
Oblique attacks with midnight's moon fraudulently to frill
The escapades of the Menads, haunting those bloody parts,
Is not, never can be, quite what Poetry sets out to instil!'

I found several cherubs to back this involved assertion.
I then said: 'What I meant, my friends, to make trebly clear
Was the extraordinary cleverness that resides in a reversion
To the sweetmeats of the ages, the bon-bons that are Fancy's
        bread.
And if you can once tap that old sugared harvest, and make
        men hear
In a sage's shell the picnicking of the distant, hungry dead,
You have them perfectly frenzied; they forget fashion: they
        are too amazed to fear.'

After this there was a long silence. You heard nothing but
        boys biting their nails.
Burke had a maudlin squint as he looked sideways at the dresser.

'When you said *shut books* in connection with Keats.'
    —But most flattened their tails
Beneath their buttocks: thinking, no doubt, on such wild
    ground the less said the besser!

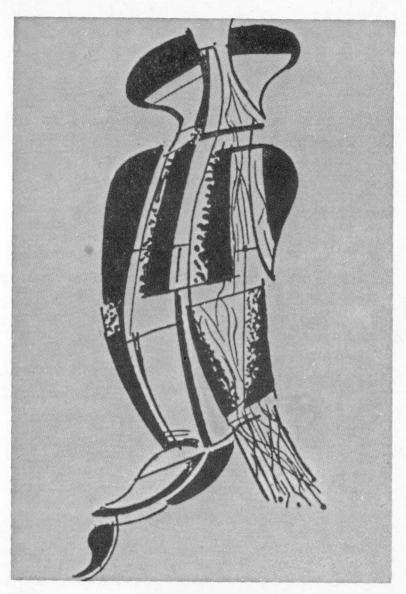

THE SONG OF THE
MILITANT
ROMANCE

THE SONG OF THE MILITANT ROMANCE

i.

Again let me do a lot of extraordinary talking.
Again let me do a lot!
Let me abound in speeches—let me abound!—publicly polyglot.
Better a blind word to bluster with—better a bad word than
    none lieber Gott!
Watch me push into my witch's vortex all the Englishman's got
To cackle and rattle with—you catch my intention?—to be
    busily balking
The tongue-tied Briton—that is my outlandish plot!

To put a spark in his damp peat—a squib for the Scotchman—
Starch for the Irish—to give a teutonic-cum-Scot
Breadth to all that is slender in Anglo-cum-Oxfordshire-Saxony,
Over-pretty in Eire—to give to this watery galaxy
A Norseman's seasalted stamina, a dram of the Volsung's salt
    blood.

ii.

As to the trick of prosody, the method of conveying the matter,
Frankly I shall provoke the maximum of saxophone clatter.
I shall not take 'limping' iambics, not borrow from Archilochous
His 'light-horse gallop', nor drive us into a short distich that
    would bog us.
I shall *not* go back to Skeltonics, nor listen to Doctor Guest.
I know with my bold Fourteener I have the measure that suits
    us best.
I shall drive the matter along as I have driven it from the first,
My peristalsis is well-nigh perfect in burst upon well-timed
    burst—
I shall drive my coach and four through the strictest of hippical
    treatises.
I do not want to know too closely the number of beats it is.
So shipwreck the nerves to enable the vessel the better to float.
This cockle shell's what it first was built for, and a most sea-
    worthy boat.
At roll-call *Byron Dominus* uttered at a fool-school,
Shouted by scottish ushers, caused his lordship to sob like a
    fool,

Yet Byron was the first to laugh at the over-sensitive Keats
'Snuffed out by an article', those were the words. A couple of
    rubber teats
Should have been supplied beyond any question to these over-
    touchy pets—
For me, you are free to spit your hardest and explode your
    bloody spleen
Regarding my bold compact Fourteener, or my four less than
    fourteen.

iii.

So set up a shouting for me! Get a Donnybrook racket on!
Hound down the drowsy latin goliaths that clutter the lexicon—
Send a contingent over to intone in our battle-line—
Wrench the trumpet out of the centre of a monkish leonine—
Courtmartial the stripling slackers who dance in the dull
    Rhyme Royal—
Send staggering out all the stammerers who stick round as
    Chaucer's foil—
Dig out the dogs from the doggerel of the hudibrastic couplet—
Hot up the cold-as-mutton songbirds of the plantagenet cabinet!
Go back to the Confessor's palace and distangle some anglo-
    saxon,
And borrow a bellow or two from the pictish or from the
    Manxman.
Set all our mother-tongue reeling, with the eruption of obsolete
    vocables,
Disrupt it with all the grammars, that are ground down to
    cement it—with obstacles
Strew all the cricket pitches, the sleek tennis-lawns of our
    tongue—
Instal a nasty cold in our larynx—a breathlessness in our lung!

iv.

But let me have silence always, in the centre of the shouting—
That is essential! Let me have silence so that no pin may drop
And not be heard, and not a whisper escape us for all our
    spouting,
Nor the needle's scratching upon this gramophone of a circular
    cosmic spot.
Hear me! Mark me! Learn me! Throw the mind's ear open—

Shut up the mind's eye—all will be music! What
Sculpture of sound cannot—what cannot as a fluid token
Words—that nothing else cannot!

                              v.
But when the great blind talking is set up and thoroughly got
        going—
When you are accustomed to be stunned—
When the thunder of this palaver breaks with a gentle soughing
Of discreet Zephyrs, or of dull surf underground—
Full-roaring, when sinus sinus is outblowing,
Backed up by a bellow of sheer blarney loudest-lunged—
That is the moment to compel from speech
That hybrid beyond language—hybrid only words can reach.

                              vi.
Break out word-storms!—a proper tongue-burst! Split
Our palate down the middle—shatter it!
Give us hare-lip and cross us with a seal
That we may emit the most ear-splitting squeal!
Let words forsake their syntax and ambit—
The dam of all the lexicons gone west!—
Chaos restored, why then by such storms hit
The brain can mint its imagery best.
Whoever heard of perfect sense or perfect rhythm
Matching the magic of extreme verbal schism?

                             vii.
Swept off your feet, be on the look out for the pattern.
It is the chart that matters—the graph is everything!
In such wild weather you cannot look too closely at 'em—
Cleave to the abstract of this blossoming.
I shall, I perhaps should say, make use of a duplicate screen—
An upper and a lower (the pattern lies between)
But most observe the understrapper—the second-string.
The counterpart's the important—keep your eye on the copy—
What's plainest seen is a mere buffer. But if that's too shoppy,
Just say to yourself—'He talks around the compass
To get back at last to the thing that started all the rumpus!'

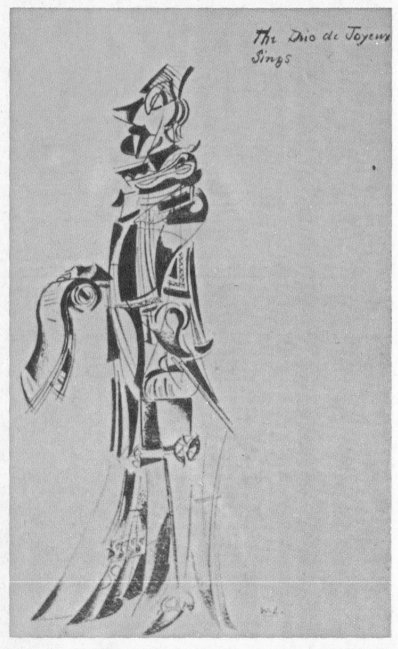

The Duc de Joyeux Sings (not previously published)

viii.

Do not expect a work of the classic canon.
Take binoculars to these nests of camouflage—
Spy out what is *half-there*—the page-under-the-page.
Never demand the integral—never completion—
Always what is fragmentary—the promise, the presage—
Eavesdrop upon the soliloquy—stop calling the spade spade—
Neglecting causes always in favour of their effects—
Reading between the lines—surprising things half-made—
Preferring shapes spurned by our intellects.
Plump for the thing, however odd, that's ready to do duty for
    another.
Sooner than one kowtowing to causation and the living-image
    of its mother.

ix.

Do your damnedest! Be yourself! Be an honest-to-goodness
    sport!
Take all on trust! Shut up the gift-nag's mouth! Batten upon
    report!
And you'll hear a great deal more, where a sentence breaks in
    two,
Believe me, than ever the most certificated school-master's
    darlings do!
When a clause breaks down (that's natural, for it's been probably
    overtaxed)
Or the sense is observed to squint, or in a dashing grammatical
    tort,
You'll find more of the stuff of poetry than ever in stupid
    syntax!

I sabotage the sentence! With me is the naked word.
I spike the verb—all parts of speech are pushed over on their
    backs.
I am the master of all that is half-uttered and imperfectly heard.
Return with me where I am crying out with the gorilla and the
    bird!

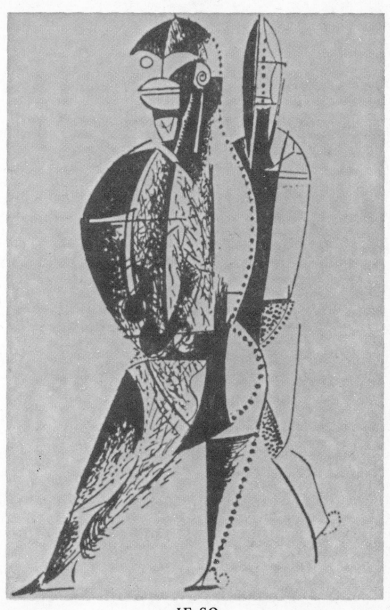

IF SO
THE MAN YOU ARE

i.

I'm no He-man you know, I'm not a He.
I'm not a chesty fellow that says *Gee*!
I'm not you know a guy that lives on pep.
I'm not a red-blood person who snaps *Yep*!
You know I've never hunted ovibos,
Nor caribou. I'd make a rotten boss
For any 'outfit'. Oh you know I'm not
Clever with Winchester or cooking-pot.
A Tempyo statuette perhaps, the Monk Ganjin,
Perhaps a patina laid very thin,
An affair of Han or T'ang, lacquered Mitsuda,
Or the brackets of a japanese pagoda—
Those things are in my line. I am very sure
I should never make a Nansen or McClure.
Forgive my frankness girls! I'm not quite yet
So destitute of manners to forget
What to sex-urge is due, film-etiquette,
What to Garbo, what to Crawford's curls.
I'm sorry if I've been too brutal girls!

ii.

I'm not the man that lifts the broad black hat.
I'm not the man's a *preux*, clichéed for chat.
I'm not the man that's sensitive to sex.
I'm not the fair Novello of the Waacs.
I'm not at breaking wind behind a hand
Too good. I'm not when hot the man that fanned
His cheek with a mouchoir. I'm not that kind.
I'm not a sot, but water leaves me blind,
I'm not too careful with a drop of Scotch,
I'm not particular about a blotch.
I'm not alert to spy out a blackhead,
I'm not the man that minds a dirty bed.
I'm not the man to ban a friend because
He breasts the brine in lousy bathing-drawers.
I'm not the guy to balk at a low smell,
I'm not the man to insist on asphodel.
This sounds like a He-fellow don't you think?
It sounds like that. I drink, I belch, I stink.

iii.

The man I am to live and to let live.
The man I am to forget and to forgive.
The man I am to turn upon my heel
If neighbours crude hostility reveal.
The man I am to stand a world of pain.
The man I am to turn my back on gain.
The man I am somewhat to overdo
The man's part—to be simple, and brave and true.
The man I am to twist my coat about
A beggar in a cold wind. Clout for clout,
I am the man to part with more than most—
I am the perfect guest, the perfect host.
The man I am (don't take this for a boast)
To tread too softly, maybe, if I see
A dream's upon my neighbour's harsh tapis.
The man I am to exact what is due to men,
The man to exact it only with the pen—
The man I am to let the machete rust,
The man I am to cry—Dust to the dust!
'The Word commands our Flesh to Dust'—that's me!
I am the man to shun Hamlet's soliloquy.

iv.

'Not the machete!' cried the young marine.
'Not with the sword!' I echoed. But its sheen
Lights up our underworld. The comets of pistols
Flash in our underworld. Fokkers and Bristols
Egg-dropping. The bomb-shit from their arses
Leaves its red trail among the fungus-masses.
'Not the machete!' screamed the youthful sailor.
'No. Bullets now!' I answered like a saviour:
'I heard he was with you boy, so I blew over.'
And Death was there indeed, bailiff and drover.
I beat it up-town. Death was there as well.
I beat it back, from one to the other hell.
'*Shoot* me!' the sea-soldier screamed. '*Not* the machete!'
But Death had other ideas. He's not so matey—
He looks at things in a different light to us.
What he does he likes doing without fuss.

If in the jungle the knife-blade has flashed,
Then *that* is the weapon: so with that he slashed.

v.

You can see from this the sort of man I am.
The tenderfoot sea-trooper gets his ham
Sliced, and I am against it all the time.
I have no words with sudden-death to rhyme.
Against shikar, and against Bela Kun,
Against all deeds beneath that bloody moon.
I am the apostle of an ancient peace,
Even spurn the provocation of my fleas.
I am the man that holds his hand. I am
The quixote-fingered mild-horned coptic ram.
With every gentle thing I would consort—
Even *gentlemen* (if not so prone to sport).
I am the tender moon upon the stream,
I am the shadow just above the dream—
(A hiccup brought this tirade to an end,
Which did throughout its course archly impend,
A good He-hiccup which dispelled that scene,
Illumined by those moons' assorted sheen).

vi.

Now come all ye who live in England's span
And tell me if I'm not a proper man.
A bollocky Bill, a mild-horned coptic ram.
And yet I'm all that is the sheer reverse
Of horsey He-man antics. Verse for verse
I can stand toe to toe with Chapman—or
With Humbert Wolfe or Kipling or Tagore!
I link my arm with the puff-armlets of Sweet Will,
I march in step with Pope, support Churchill.
The tudor song blossoms again when I speak.
With the cavaliers I visit, with Donne I am dark and meek.
With Cleveland I coin phrases—Inca buds
From a tree blasted. I am devout with Isaac Watts.
I am the genuine article, no doubt.
I drown my whispers in a libidinous shout.
I am hoarse with telling men to take more care.
P'raps that gives me my hoarse He-mannish air!

vii.

I once was lifted on a bitter moon,
And tossed into the ranges around noon.
Looking about me I caught sight of two
Sad rustics, who within these pastures grew.
I counted them, and found that they were twain.
Men stopped them and then parked them in the rain.
Believe it or not, I was sorry for those men,
Indeed I was: I loathed their regimen.
I went up to them. 'Brothers,' I said, 'I'm here
Like you napoo?' I inspired them with some fear.
Seeing that, I raised my hat. I left them alone.
As I withdrew I heard a double groan,
From the four lungs of the two chests—but 'twas a natural thing!
What song that they had ever sung could they unsing?
—I am the man thus brought in contact with
Misery, to see it, and make of it a myth.
No hollow man, a tin pulse in his wrist—
I have always thought it better to resist
From childhood up, and have done with every fear.
About *nothing* am I absolutely clear.

viii.

The man I can when others cannot be—
When they're most mannish, why that's not for me!
(Because I am so modest I'm so frank.
I know how the class-conscious crab my rank).
Now when I'm up in arms others are not,
When I'm most male they are a softish lot.
They puff their chests when I deflate my own.
They stick their jaws out when my own jawbone
Is tucked back in my neck. So there you are!
There is a time to spar and not to spar.
My time to spar is the reverse of men's.
They are often cocky, but when I'm a cock they're hens!
Devil a bit can I catch up with what
I think behind me, or consider hot
What leaves me cold. I cannot be the man
To sport in summer gauntlets of astrakan.
I cannot be the man therefore to be
What a man is as a conventional He.

ix.

Stumble upon this block. You wangle when
You come to seize the bright strap-hanging pen,
In an overcoat-pocket. (This is the block you've seen
Midway to the big sporting guillotine.)
Come now, crestfallen! I'll cut off your crest.
Come now, crude angel, I'll give you of my best!
I'm not half the man to bivouac just half-way.
No half-way house beyond the frosty bay
Is a stone beacon. Yesterday's enough.
Come now, my curlew! The icepack's up to snuff,
And the young ice is strong. Come now, Bellerophon
Spliced with the Twilight. My little sun-myth, come!
Let us together hunt the Chimaera. Look
Leonine-headed near this arctic brook.
When and for which? Because when all is done
And said and left unsaid I'm the first fearless one
To have faced the pressure ridges and gone out.
There are three standard manners of dugout
To be made, with a lot of other ways. What then?
I can write Limbo-lingo with the best of men.
There's no man can blot out the sense—there's none
Has a better anaesthetic in his gun.
I've travelled on far thinner ice than this.
There's nothing I can't do without a kiss.

x.

Come on my curly party. I'll be frank!
Why should I mount the bridge where Amos stank
And suffered? A pox on the vice of beds.
Give me a sunflower and I'll chop their heads.
(That's where the chicken got the chopper, lad.
Upon his curly sunflower discus pat.)
Now look you beagles when the bugles blow
And the waves splash, with harriers below
Seek shelter in the bowels of the ship,
And hunt the Snark for the remainder of the trip.
There's safety in numbers. Never forget when aft
To clamour for Spratt's Biscuits and a raft.
—Rats leave the sinking ship. The rats and you
Breasting those sterner waters, when it blew

A polar gale, will up with both your tails
And paddle off. (Rat-hunters through the gales
Fraternize rodents. There's great safety in
Numbers, and repulse the darkling fin.
Up mammals! when confronted with a fish.
—The Thought is but the bastard of the Wish.)
Come now my curly griffin and be friends.
Show me the Rubber Stamp. I'll make amends.
What's Bellerophon to me or I to him—
To Hecuba, to Troy's deep-chested cream
Of luckless warriors. What to me the scent
Of battle? Of the first Paris frowning sent?

xi.

Sperm of the Earth! Better unmentioned be!
I had a close call from the percussion of the sea.
Castor and Pollux fought for me throughout
The far campaigns, under my eagles. Drought
Lifted me bodily and thirst connived
With scurvy—many a good man has unlived,
In conjunction with nephritis. It's been bad
From first to last! Excuse me if I'm sad.
Going one better, I thrust out my hand
Beckoned Chimaera. Not the man to understand
Am I, this lamb, and feline dragonette.
(Excuse me if I harp upon this pet.)
I never was a lion—of modest mark.
The powers-that-be were frightened by my bark.
I scorn the helvetian body of the goat.
All that was left me was the dragon's coat.
Sperm of the Earth! Better to be *no one*.
Who is it that you *need* to be, Son of the Sun?

xii.

At this point let us become more *personal*—
What do you think—a proper sporting spell!
Come down to earth with me and rummage round
In things as concrete as our well-pegged pound,
Round fourteen shillings: things as far apart
As the economic history of art,
And the great laws that hedge the life of Dr Fell,

That admirable physician! Let us tell
Each other stories of the dark campaigns
That dominate the output of our brains.
And for that purpose I will call upon
A powerful ghost, as well up as any don
In his particular subject—introduce
(This is a piece of really first-class news)
A great professional Outcast of the Pen,
A happy swordsman, a modest gentleman.
I refer, of course, to Mister Enemy.
His shadow over everything I see,
A hostile shadow—I scarcely think I blame
This portent for his habits, or his name.
Ours *is* a clownish age. If so the man
You be to understand it then you can
Scarcely be other than a Man in an Iron Mask
Or choose but choose a most invidious task.—
Henceforth the voice you hear is the deep growl—
The mask, if any, the notorious scowl—
Of Enemy Number One. He has been shown
The text so far, and will take up the tone
And carry on, in characteristic style,
With personalities our smile outsmile.

ENTER THE ENEMY
(*cloaked, masked, booted, and with gauntlets
of astrakan*)

ENEMY INTERLUDE

xiii.
SHOUTS

Am I too dangerous, that no man can let
This 'wild beast' out, but keep it as a pet?
Must I on charity be so sustained,
And never be unwittingly unchained?
Must I be given *nothing*, lest I take
Too much from the world's *trop-plein*? Fake after fake,
Encouraged, must usurp the place is mine?
And yet had I demanded a gold mine,
Or aimed to be dictator of the West,
I could not be regarded as a pest
More than I am by asphalt-inkslinger
Alike, and in-the-manger monied cur—
Nor more askance if my pen were a sword
Excalibur, itching to strike abroad!
What is it that men fear beyond everything?
Obviously an open person. Bring
One of us 'truthful ones' too near, their nests
Would be unfeathered. Experience invests
Us with such terrors, us whose tongues are clean,
It is rarely in the high-places we are seen.
If such as I were made too famous, oh
What would he not be doing here below!
Hence very aged men—else ruffians tried—
Are puffed and boosted, flattered and glorified.
The Shaws of this world, they are *safe*, that's it!
In the toothless head there's no danger for the bit.
So there you have (in this political age)
The secret of the dishonour of the sage—
The one that's young enough to have some teeth,
The one that's suspected honest underneath.

xiv.

The man I am to blow the bloody gaff
If I were given platforms? The riff-raff
May be handed all the trumpets that you will.
Not so the golden-tongued. The window-sill
Is all the pulpit they can hope to get,

Of a slum-garret, sung by Mistinguette,
Too high up to be heard, too poor to attract
Anyone to their so-called 'scurrilous' tract.
What wind an honest mind advances? Look
No wind of sickle and hammer, of bell and book,
No wind of any party, or blowing out
Of any mountain hemming us about
Of 'High Finance', or the foothills of same.
The man I am who does *not* play the game!
Of those incalculable ones I am
Not to be trusted with free-speech to damn,
To be given enough rope—just enough to hang.
To be hobbled in a dry field. As the bird sang
Who punctured poor Cock Robin, by some sparrow
Condemned to be shot at with toy bow and arrow.
You will see how it stands with all of those
Who strong propensities for truth disclose.
It's no use buddy—you are for it boy
If not from head to foot a pure alloy!
If so the man you are that lets the cat
Out of the bag, you're a marked fellow and that's flat.

xv.

If so the man you are to let the cat
Outside, expect your beer a little flat!
If so the man you are to keep it in
Always, then never worry. You will win!
Should things go slow at first, they're watching you—
To see if you're cat-conscious! If you say boo
To goose or serpent. But keep pussy down,
And out of sight, the finest house in town
Is yours for the asking and you'll be a knight
If you want to be—if the *cat* is out of sight!
They *must* see where the bloody cat will jump
All said and done. If with a scandalous bump
Or deftly on all fours. *You* are the cat
You see, in that connection—a puss to pat
Or to garrot. I'm positive you're that—
I mean the former. If you're up to scratch
No one on you will be a mouldy patch.—
If so the man you are to let the puss

Out of the knapsack, you're a simple goose.
You must know who your enemy is my god
By this time, or you're a very brainless sod!

xvi.

If so the man you are to pick up sticks
Then why expect to have a house of bricks?
Merchant of fag-ends, if that's what you are,
Why should they give you a full-sized cigar?
If so the man you are commissionaire
Stock-still to stand for a pittance, why that's fair,
If so the man you are! I can't see why
Whacked from your hobo-holding you need cry.
Balata or gold, if so the man you are
The optimist-prospector, spit on your star:
Who would hand out a hoot if such a man
Had fits of grief? I don't see how *I* can.
If so the man you be to set your cap
At Croesus' crooked daughters you're a low chap.
For you may marry gold, or ships or rubber
Only if you're a proper money-grubber,
If so the man you be—I'm betting boy
You're not that cold, well-turned, steel-hammered toy.
If so the man you were, upon my lice,
I'd not give you this spate of good advice!—
Since so the man you are to turn your back
Upon the baton, so I think, in your knapsack.

xvii.

If so the man you are commissionaire,
If so the man *marchand de mégots* there,
If so the man you are, *oh merde alors*!
If so the man to bang each taxi-door,
If so the man bemedalled, a 'man's-man' too,
If so the man you are to *all* men true,
If so you are the servant-man, why then,
If so the man (a scarecrow among men)
If such the man you are, these words we waste,
If so the man by nature's hand disgraced.
If so the man you be for the back-seat,
If so the man out of the hand to eat,

A fetch-and-carry fellow to salute,
If so the man that's just above the brute.
If so the man like the majority of men,
If so the man that's envious of the pen,
If so the man you are of the other cheek,
If so the man that's venomous and sleek,
If so the man that's Everyman—these words,
If so a man, we throw to the dicky-birds!

xviii.

If so some man when I began to be
I looked beyond the confines of the sea.
I thought my books by German and by Frog
Would be read in deutsch and frankish—Britain's log
For Nineteen Twenty-Six and the years just after.
That naivety must provoke our present laughter.
(I had reckoned without our british business-men):
They have never passed the frontiers of the pen
I wrote them with, except my Hitler Book.
That got through the blockade of boob and crook.
A surprising feat, it swam the Nordic Sea,
And planted its swastika in High Germany.
But lo upon the sidewalks of New York
I am now of the same standing as Montalk,
If that, of course. Spluttered in Cabala
It reaches me, the hiss of menacing blah.
Meanwhile, excluded, *Snooty Baronet*,
Felt the full boycott, it is not sold yet,
Nor ever will be. These are long vendettas.
A peculiar people, neither forgivers nor forgetters.
All that I know is that my agents write
'Your Hitler Book has harmed you'—in a night,
Somewhat like Byron—only I waken thus
To find myself not famous but infamous.

xix.

But what have I done in this most mild brochure,
Depicting german manners, to be sure,
Which are so political, what man can write
Unpartisan, without much of 'Left' and 'Right'?
If so the man you are to provoke this hate
I ask myself to what my crimes relate.
High politics I shun—I gave but an impression
Of the Berlin scene, in very impartial fashion.
Are we forbidden (and if so by whom)
To mention a man in Kun's or Lenin's room,
Except in belittlement, column after column,
A 'Germany puts the Clock back' sort of volume?
I am puzzled by this ubiquitous virulence.
I ask myself the Whither and the Whence.
Is it not fitter that the Brit should know
The sort of sunlessness makes Hitlers grow?
I like the german nation. If they have faults
From the *cause* thereof every sane mind revolts.
They do but answer persecution with
It's like. What then? Recall flamboyant myth
To warm their hearts at, every other fuel
Denied them—they revive mensur, they duel!
These are but human gestures after all.
From wall-game gazing a yet greater fall
Our anglo-saxon Humpty Dumpty yet
May take—what would your worship care to bet?

XX.

[xx.]

The house of Kippenberg, *Insel-Verlag*,
A great *rheindeutsches* book-firm and *sans blague*,
Abruptly cabled to an agent here
Asking in terms both liberal and clear
For contracts, german world-rights, yes a mass
Offer for all my books, starting with *Childermass*.
What happened? Need you ask. All that I know
Is that, as suddenly, they ceased to glow
With the same incandescence. All I can guess
Some influence set itself to unimpress.
A cable came to cancel everything.
But, most significant, the inner ring
To the number I think of four of the boosted pets
Of a certain London firm my contract gets—
A firm with whom I have some slight connection,
A firm not best pleased with the unique selection,
Of a writer kept outside the pale in Britain,
A dangerous writer it was their task to sit on
And keep in servitude upon a pittance—
And keep his 'mailed fist' safe within their mittens!
A firm of 'the highest standing', with whom alas
I have some slight connection.—'What a farce'!
Why not at all! We 'authors', as such call us,
Are always ready to oblige such crawlers
Within our shirts with a little handy gore—
We merely *write* the books, we do no more,
All said and done. We are only the fool-authors.
That's why the likes of us, if Fritz would launch us,
Soon learn that there is many a dirty slip
Betwixt the outlandish cup and the british lip.

xxi.

Linati, that fine critic of Milan,
Surveying authors 'americo-anglican',
Treats of Your's Truly in a sensible way.
A 'poeta maladetto' of today
Am I: he notes the suppressive tendency,
As what outsider would not? 'Anthology
Excludes him', I am even excluded too
From all official mention—all except *Who's Who*.

I am an 'outcast' and a man 'maudit'.
But how romantic! Don't you envy me?
A sort of Villon, bar the gallows: but
Even there I may be accommodated yet.
Why yes it's very jolly to be picked
As the person not so much as to be kicked,
As the person who de facto *is not there*,
As the person relegated to the dark back-stair.
'Outcast' is good, in a system of shark and gull,
Where all that's 'illustrious' is also Untouchable!
A solitary honour. To be he
For whose benefit *unmentionability*
Has been invented, as a new order of the Dead
Who yet exist—an even forlorner head
Borne upon his trunk than the shorn skull
Of a monk vowed to his pastimes void and null.
Suffer embargo, live upon boycott, why
It's very jolly! But what's the wherefore, what the why?
So I get your meaning, but alas demur;
For, odd as it may seem, I'd much prefer
From time to time to earn a little cash—
The 'necessary' to work, not cut a dash.

xxii.

I have a lot to say about myself,
Anent low matters centering in pelf?
'Must you remind us that all art is trade?
What has the artist's *self* to do with what he has made?'
Upon *that* you may be enlightened on the spot.
No artist can 'be himself' *and* boil-the-pot.
Withhold from him all sources of supply
Infallibly that art-man comes to die.
If, subtler than that, you sabotage
His efforts to expand himself at large
And hold him back from markets and from men,
Abroad, you've got him screwed down in his pen.
It's no joke if the New York market's blocked,
Aside from fame, if that big door is locked,
And Germans dissuaded too from making me
An english author 'known in Germany',
That is a shrewd ill-turn to say the least.

The excuse is I'm a sort of savage beast—
Too easy is that explanation though.
Nor will the *pure-commerce* cry exactly do.
(There is no pure-commerce as there is no 'pure art'.
Romance unbleakens the most hard-boiled heart.)
There are more things in heaven and earth than these,
But do not ask me to describe them please.
It is enough that no man you can name
Has had so much to huckster for mere fame.
So I'm driven to conclude there's something else.
But what it is I cannot guess—it smells
Extremely like a rat, but what's the use
Of hunting this fishy rodent where it chews!

xxiii.

Now, we all go to war with bomb and gas
State against state, that's understood. Whereas
What no 'man-of-the-world' will yet admit
Is that this recognized official fit
Of spleen is duplicated in whatever sense
Upon the private plane—that is nonsense!
In this fair world of 'gentlemen's agreements',
A lawcourtly world, where for their fat fees fence
Scurrilous bravos, it would be a pure outrage
So much as to suggest small wars we wage—
With all that 'war' takes with it of boycott and debt,
Of strategy, false news, spy-traps baited and set—
With for our poison-gas our septic breath,
And writs for bombs; honour in place of death!
All these hidalgos are the soul of honour,
And always in *some* way a munificent donor!
A man too poor his honour to defend
Is a dishonourable man unto the end.
This world of 'gentlemen's agreements' none
Admits too poor to be a 'gentleman'.
And there are tags to go with this brave system—
The wisdom of the crow, if it be wisdom.
Collar a cutpurse, he'll say that you're 'suspicious'.
Retaliate upon a crook, why then you're 'vicious'.
Or call the smirking bluff of the pomp-monger
He spits out 'cad'! He marks you down for hunger.

The world of 'faux-bonhommes' is that of the fake
    'monsieurs',
And that of the cheapjacks that of the muzzled seers.

xxiv.

Another cogent argument when one
Unmasks a slight, is—'You're *too good* my son!
Good writers naturally annoy the fool,
And you are no exception to the rule!'
This is a jolly clever argument.
It covers almost *every* incident.
To this trick I take off my hat. First class
For isolating merit from the mass.
The 'penman's clubs' where Baerleins, Baums and Goldings
Transact their business and stake out their holdings,
It is only fit should be shrouded from the eye
Of that strange sport the self-styled 'Enemy'.
But in such haunts the money changes fists—
The 'needful' and the 'ready', harmless grists
For all those creaking mills that turn and give
Innocuous 'penman' wherewithal to live.
And still and all, we know the invisible prison
Where men are jailed off—men of *dangerous* vision—
In impalpable dark cages of neglect,
Invisible walls by self-protective sect
Or cabal against the Individual built,
(At best with honorifics and lip-service killed).—
Well understanding tactics such as these,
Conversant with historic instances,
You can hardly blame an 'Enemy' who forestalls
Such treatment and puts up his own high walls.
You can scarcely grumble if an impersonal seer
Is doubled with an efficient pamphleteer!
He has *his* business, too, all said and done,
To nurse and peddle—the Business of the Sun!

xxv.

Ah ah! Ah ah! The Business of the Sun!
A passport occupation!—so it might run
On the same principle as Borrow's pets.
'Business of Egypt', muttered the gypsy wits,

To account for goings and comings hard to explain.—
I peddle solar bombshells in the rain.
(I seek no substitute for worldly pomp—
I accept a rented coffin in a swamp.
Persona grata in a few freak shops,
On the distaff side I'm well in with the cops—
I know a Dogberry who lurks at the street corner
Got up to represent my little friend Jack Horner).—

(*'Jack Horner' was a cue—a second shade*
Dwarfish and fat, of stale cigarsmoke made,
With a surly swagger joins the first to ask
A batch of questions, taking the first to task.)

'*Insel-Verlag*—under the caption of the Sun
'Must that be entered? What have those book-firms done
'To pervert solar energy, in perverting you?
'What swastika is that you planted and flew?
'Why do you call the North Sea "Nordic" now?
'New York you seem to regard as your milch-cow.
'Do you want fame for Phoebus or for self?
'Do you say Liberty is on the shelf?
'Are you quite sure, odd bagman, your valise
'Holds solar energy, or only fleas?
'Is *Snooty Baronet* that dirty book
'I once for D. B. Wyndham's jests mistook?
'What is your solar business, which your bank—
'Accredited to the zodiac, what's your rank?
'Do you claim to be immune as diplomat,
'Or Dogberry or what? When you outsat
'All others at the sittings of the moot,
'Were you afraid your scheme would be pooh-poohed?'

xxvi.

And I to answer this tart questionnaire
In a fashion becoming a courteous bugbear.
'No sir' I gravely answer 'that's not it.
'If I were selling soap, or selling wit,
'I would not talk of *business*, I'd be shy
'Regarding L.S.D.—As it is energy
'I peddle I am not ashamed to refer

'To the interference I encounter, sir!
'A hundred thousand demijohns I'd hide:
'But not the pale tresses of the solar bride.'
It's very difficult indeed, of course,
To show that this is not a *personal* force.
I do not beg subscriptions for the sun—
I come to levy imposts! One by one
I get into a row with angry persons
Who cast upon my functions tart aspersions.
Masks made of bast are useful, a ripsnorter
Bursts on our faces, full of angry water
And forked electricity. What is the use
The indignant elements when they recuse
To menace with sunstroke? I've had quite enough
Of heated argument about my stuff.
The long and the short of this is I am not
A doll of set responses in a fixed cot.
I go about and use my eyes, my tongue
Is not for sale—a little loosely slung
Perhaps but nothing more. I esteem my rôle
To be grand enough to excuse me, on my soul,
From telling lies at all hours of the day!
Of saying the thing that is not, Swift would say.
If I am armed with bright invective, rare
That is I agree—but mine is a *dangerous* affair.

xxvii.

(*And now begins a snooty tit-for-tat,*
The Enemy rejoinder's very pat,
But entirely circumspect—the other shadow
Proving himself a thoroughgoing cad though.)
'Are you the man that was the person sent
'To trip up our puppets with your argument?'—
'If so I was the man I'd not look twice
'At all the tortured cohorts of your mice!'—
'If so you be the authenticated sage
'Of our epoch, why aren't you all the rage?'—
'Because, old mole, "the rage" is in your keeping:
'Because *"the rage" c'est moi*! With Warwick Deeping
'You do your work, or the late Galsworthy, you see.
'Because you are so the man to boost the flea!'—

'If so the man you are to go to bed
'With a painted pillow, were you not better dead!'—
'If so the man I were, then that's correct.
'If so the man to sell me to your sect.'—
'I think you are the man I caught at cheating
'With the whiskered card—the cutlassed King retreating?'—
'My prestidigitation with *the Knave*
'You may have noticed, the whole pack to save!
'Set a thief to catch a thief, you know!'—
'Are you the player trumped our Ukiyo?'—
'The Floating World is none of my concern!'—
'Are you the coward made off with the voter's urn?'—
'If so the man you ask, that shall I be!'—
'Were you the man that stole my cypher-key?'—
'Was I the man defaced your privy wall?'
'Were *you* the man conceived that monstrous ball?'—
'Was I the man the man that breathed his last?'—
'Were *you* that dead man scooting down the blast?'—
'Was I the man foozled at playing Auction?'—
'Were *you* that partner with the crass concoction?'—
'Was I the lion that looked in on your toilet?'
'Were *you* that tawny vermin! You may boil yet!
'You filled my bath-closet with an illegal roar,
'And threatened my footman with a rampant paw.'

xxviii.

'Mine is a *dangerous* errand, do you hear?'
'Enough of these insults, you intolerable seer!'
'I·shoot from the hip, but can you really wonder?'
'You scurrilous pastmaster in blood and thunder!'
'Mine is a grim affair—I'm not a thug.'
'How dare you raise this most unseemly fug!'
'An ex-post-facto picture shows me how
'I might have avoided that distracted cow.'
'Ah would it had struck deeper with its horn!'
'Luckily the slight cornada was ill-born.'
'But had it reached another inch *bien-né*!'
'I wonder how you rank your own birthday!'
'I'll see you're never mentioned in *my* Press!'
'I should not be in any case!'—'Disgrace!'
'Blot on your country and the human race!'
'Which do you patronize for preference, though—

'The genre humain, or nation? May I know?'
'You know I'd die for *every* nation once—
'Yank, Scotch or Polish—I'd die twice for France!'
'Are you the man I saw in Hyde Park or
'Richmond perhaps, run in at night?'—'You boor!
'Hitter below the belt, spy on your betters!
'You scandal in the world of life and letters!'
'In which you shine, of course, drunken with money,
'Smug poet of the land of milk and honey!'
'I'll see you have your photo in *my* organs!'
'*And* grace the "special list" of J. P. Morgan's—
'*And* have the moon, and mounts and marvels ditto!'
'You'll swing for this—you're wife's a merry widow!'
'Maybe. But still I'll have with you a *bet*.'
'That I'll be even with your rude tongue yet!'
'Why no, but that you *must*, being but half-real,
'One fine day overreach your crazy zeal!'

(EXIT ANTAGONIST OF ENEMY, BOILING AND
FREEZING WITH INDIGNATION)
(*The Enemy watches the retreating heckler—swollen
to unusual proportions by the blood he is always sucking
into the gorged cistern of his person: The Enemy stoops
slightly, the better to observe this paranoiac interloper
shaking the dust off his feet beneath the Enemy portico.
Then the Enemy sits down once more and plies his trade.*)

xxix.

Well well well!!!—a dirty piece of work—
Come out of the murk, gone back into the murk!
As sure as my name's Faust, that's one of the worst
That ever on my deadened senses burst.
He brought an odour with him that went well
With the congested passions of his dead hell,
Built in the early days of human spleen,
Concocted of a frausty discipline.
He had a waggle of his hinder parts
As if shaken by the combustion of dud farts.
He had an apoplectic barber's block,
From always keeping under key and lock
And walling-up his septic rages. Scarred

With carbuncle and pockpit, caused in part
By innate pus, and partly by mental fever—
The fake-blue-eyed professional deceiver!
He lives by force—that imperfect force that is grounded
On legal bluff, by wordslingers expounded—
Extremely artificial; always apt
To be by some brusque natural movement snapped.
Good riddance for the air's opaque with bugs
When he's about, and the bad breath of his paid thugs
Close on his heels, if not in flesh in spirit,
Is aimed to stifle unassuming merit.

(*The Enemy spits, and a small green flame darts up
from the gothic parquet. He looks at the spot where the
flame has emerged, and then spits again. A second flame-
let gushes from the floor.*)

XXX.

You now solicit a few enemy thrusts
At the stock poets' thickly bay-leaved busts.
Ranged in that portrait-place, of marble and clay,
August with the as-yet unwithered bay.
I seem to note a roman profile bland,
I hear the drone from out the cactus-land:
That must be the poet of the Hollow Men:
The lips seem bursting with a deep Amen.
I espy Ezra, bearded like the Kaiser,
And wistful Earp, like a mediaeval sizar,
The learned beneficiary of provisions,
Gone to the buttery to lubricate his visions.
And there's Roy Campbell, stiff-chested and slim,
Posed for veronicas before wild terrapin.
Moore, the sturgeon of the Hampstead Hill,
Nations of Greeks and Hebrews drives at will
Across a gothic landscape: and James Joyce
For the third time his thirteen poems deploys.
Read broods above old battles. Sacheverell
Odd bloated ghosts compelling to retell
Their famous victories. The greater Yeats,
Turning his back on Ossian, relates
The blasts of more contemporary fates.

And Richard Aldington, equipped to sing
The beauties of an impossible greek spring.
Graves, Osbert, and Sassoon, and many others,
Brothers-in-arms and pen-aborted brothers:
And Auden (most recent bust) with playground whistle:
MacDiarmid beneath a rampant thistle.—
As it's my rôle to provide the personal chord,
These names I hope some slight kick will afford.
We are not very rich in laurelled heads—
We are a little age, where the blind pygmy treads
In hypnotized crusades against all splendour,
Perverts male prowess to the middle gender.
We are a critic-company, what's more.
The Rōnin, the Wave-Men, camp in the ruined door.

(The Enemy rises and stretches, in the rôle of Dr Faustus, and smiles in our direction, and bows as if to say, 'Have I played my part to your satisfaction?' I bow to show my appreciation, let my eye rove over the cobwebs among the gothic girders, and to the clouds of hot pipe-smoke where they hang in the vaults and crypts of the roof, and back to the door. At the door I bow again, and the Enemy lifts his large black steeple-hat, resumes his seat and plies his trade. I close the door softly and descend the spiral stair.)

END OF ENEMY INTERLUDE

xxxi.

I knew you'd like the Enemy! He's the person
May pen in plastic fashion a new verse on
The *Heldenleben* and colossi's lot,
Or with his pen put penclubs on the spot.
He knows to live comes first. No bee in his bonnet
Outbuzzes any other that lands on it.
His balance is astonishing when you consider
He has never sold himself to the highest bidder,
Never has lived a week for twenty summers
Free of the drumfire of the camouflaged gunners,
Never has eaten a meal that was undramatic—
Without the next being highly problematic.
Never succumbed to panic, *kaltes blut*
His watchword, facing ahead in troubled mood.
He has been his own bagman, critic, cop, designer,
Publisher, agent, char-man and shoe-shiner.
What he has just narrated of double-dealing
Is nothing to what he could, of professional stealing,
Of the betrayal of unpublished texts to ladies,
A court d'idées, and other crimes (his fate is
Of course to be a quarry of rich pickings,
He's the bull's-eye of 'brain-pickers' like the dickens)—
Of unwelcome names bluepencilled in an article
Caught in the act, and minding not a particle
(We suffer from a strange delusion—that is
That our age is 'straighter' than was grand-daddy's!)—
Of that discrimination against all writers
Suspected of having eyes in their heads. Good fighters
When-driven-in-corners are common: but here's a fellow
Who does not wait to be trapped—an aggressive fellow!
I was sure you'd like him and that was why I brought him—
It was a piece of luck it happened that I caught him.

xxxii.

And yet this 'Enemy' counters all my song.
His is a battle all the way along.
With him the machete never seems to rust.
No room with him for thoughts of the ultimate dust.
Confucian philosophy and arms
Seem equal partners in his iron charms.

Ideal samurai, virtuous, loyal, modest,
He brings a tolerant something to the West,
That was never there before, I think, with this
Odd code of a devotion we have lost:
Samurai, yes, but with an artist crossed.
His not the tender moon above the stream!
And yet what pathos in this bitter gleam
Upon the unwanted weapons, of one grieved
To find his country gardens all unleaved
At the behest of half-men, a thought lower
Than the lowest yet, since the days of Priam or Noah—
The Gutter Men (like the Beaker Men): a mark
They will leave on everything, ghastly and dark.
The Money Men—our weakness gave them their chance.
The fault is ours—if we stalk to their voodoo dance.
If so the man you are half this to see,
You must salute this outcast Enemy—
Outcasted for refusal to conform
To the phases of this artificial storm.
If so the man he were to lift the hand,
To-morrow he would promptly be unbanned,
Saluting if the ruffian of the piece—
If saying what he knows by heart to please.

xxxiii.

I scratch the Enemy's back, do overtime,
And he with no less vigour scratches mine.
I call him Friend and he calls back at me
'Friend'. He is a gentle Enemy!
(These lonely compliments no animus
Can cause, this gentle fooling between us.)
If so the man we all were like this one
No man would need to carry a shot-gun!
A motley, of thrasonical intent,
He affects, to stage his modest argument.—
If names could bark then I think Woffington
Would bark at us. But it is dead and gone,
And only fleshless eardrums now can smash.
A bottle-companion, almost a Captain Flash
Or possible Copper Captain, or Bobadil,
Since with her voice a big house she could fill

As strident as a mercenary troop—
That's her all right, that's her uncanny whoop.
Enemy can speak softly as she could speak
With a man's roar. His bark is almost meek.
You bet your sweet life that no Beefsteak Club
Would admit Enemy to lunch or sup,
Alcoholic prophylaxis notwithstanding.
He is far too gentle for that boisterous banding.
Alarming monuments we must whitewash,
All thinking men, to guy the popular bosh.

xxxiv.

If man alive you're so the chap to care,
To arms! while yet the brave deserve the fair.
If so the man you are commissionaire,
Go back, hang up your medals on the stair,
To glimpse, at coming in, at going out,
If so the man you are with whiskered pout,
Or ambushed eyes of light sky-blue of course,
Expression a little quizzing, a little cross;
A man to be trusted with no matter what,
A sort of walking safe-deposit. Dot
And carry one, with a few simple arts—
If so a man of these resplendent parts,
A sodden lump of 'independent' meat,
Organic as a street-lamp, hard to beat
At doing nothing, a great man for your 'rights',
Who on a heavy ration 'doggedly' fights,
Observing all the rules of 'clean' warfare,
A well-paid and protesting sleepy-pear,
And who, for the King's shilling or the Queen's,
A well-groomed, costly watchdog from his teens
To sixties proves, if so the man you be,
Never so much as touched with phantasy—
A servant-man for ever and a day,
But working little for a great deal of pay—
If so the man you are, your leaders gone,
Can you survive into an age of iron?
In this political cockpit who can you face?
Yours must become a very lowly place.
Against the grain, we henceforth must discount

The sleepy people petted and 'all-found'.
Unless, unless, a class of leaders comes,
To move it from its latter-day doldrums.

**ONE-WAY
SONG**

ONE-WAY SONG

i.

Let me sing the song of the Fronts! Exhort me now to sing
Of those bold Fronts that are the screens of Everything.
In place of 'Backs of Letters', to be read
With difficulty (see Swift) put *Fronts* instead.
'Each Atom by some other struck,' Swift says,
'All Turns and Motions tries.' Let me impress
A motion upon such Atoms, causing them
To integrate, and so 'Behold a Poem'!
I would set all things whatsoever front to back,
All that go upright—by these tactics show
How the bold Fronts depend upon this knack
Of nature's—how our one-way bodies grow—
Always *Eyes-front*! Creatures of Progress! suited
Only for one-way travel, in Time bodily rooted.

ii.

Try and walk backwards: you will quickly see
How you were meant only *one-way* to be!
Attempt to gaze out of your bricked-up back:
You will soon discover what we *One-ways* lack!
Endeavour to re-occupy the Past:
Your stubborn front will force you to stand fast!
(No traffic-caption of *Sens Interdit*
Is necessary for this clearly One-Way Street.)
Address yourself to sitting down front-first—
Your joints will stop you, or your hips will burst!
Try and read backwards out of any book—
Essay to take a walk eyes-shut and not to look—
It will be useless! Only machines reverse—
All that has mind may not go arsieverse!
Creatures of Fronts we are—designed to bustle
Down paths lit by our eyes, on stilts of clockwork muscle—
And furthermore this clockwork works clockwise,
Forward on vectors traced out by our eyes.
So there you have it! How important *frontness* is
I need not labour further—even backness is frontness!

iii.

Oh to be *One-way*—yet to be said to look
'Before and after'! What bat was it mistook
The ancestral coccyx for a periscope—
Who was it handed out that *two-way* dope?
(Oh blast his eyes who took my tail to be
A spy-glass, or supposed my back could see.
That two-way stuff's in the worst taste. What's more
It saddened Shelley. I prefer Old Moore.)
DORSUM's our password, with six-foot of wall
Twixt us and pastness—a Humpty Dumpty fall
For little you or me, if we should use
Our backs for peeping-tomming. Goodie Two Shoes
Could not be goodier than little Miss One-Way
Or Master same, vowed to the Forthright-Way.

iv.

Are you young Master One-Way? Are you he!
Are you that sad identical young she,
Who is all onewaywardness, who to be salt
On Sodomitic cliffs may yet be called,
Who knows? but if that's the case I'll bet you're salted
For never looking back—from very goaheadness halted.—
Are you Miss Time-girl?—Master Clock I think!
'Habe die Ehre!' How we One-ways stink
Of progress! I could tell you by your smell!
The effluvium of progress suits you well
Allow me to say sir! (to the perfume born
Of an 'expanding universe', a bursting corn—
An ever-budding, bigger and better, system—
Where no one's ever missed a cosmic bus—or missed 'em
Only because strap-hangers blocked the portals
To get more air, the antisocial mortals—
Yet bigger and better buses every minute
Roar forth. Before you know it you are in it!
One hefty public carriage packed to the brim
With One-ways, Kruschensalted to get slim).
Stagnation has its must. But it's most odd
That *stuffy* odour all One-ways have got!
One would hardly have thought that progress such as ours
Would have made us smell like bloody hot-house flowers!

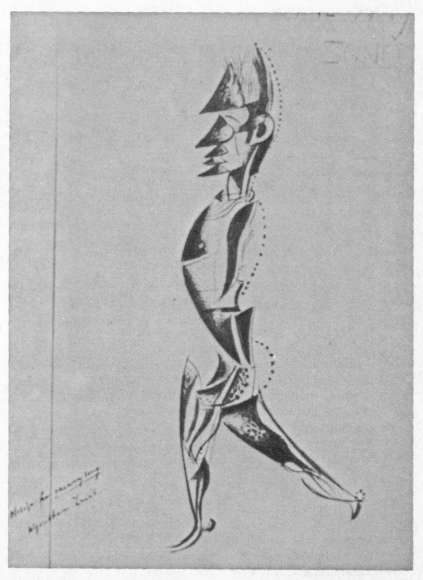

One Way Figure (not previously published)

v.

A portentous start—to take a snapshot aim
At Backs in the abstract—but you see my game—
To shoot off all the epaulettes and bustles,
To flatten out the controversial muscles
Which hint at four-armed fool-gods of the Hindu,
Furnished with dorsal duplicates for the two
Front-handed members, a peg-top of a person.
So kindly overlook my rude aspersion—
No *by-your-leave* as an 'Eyes-front' contraption
To salute your honour—'One-Way' *is* my caption,
For better or for worse. I *am* the song bird
Of the dogmatic one-way Front-Man. I exert
Each day a ton of energy on this,
Just this—to bolster up all onewayness.
Ah, once you've said *progress*!—in that little matter
I confess to being as mad as a March Hatter!

vi.

Take it from me my One-Way brother—frère
Semblable! (to link up with Baudelaire)
That 'pectus est quod facit' *us*, in sum,
Your Front, what makes *you*, makes 'theologum':
Your God's forever there under your nose,
His attributes are counted on your toes!
And what's the odds if now and then you feel
A bit mechanical and not quite 'real'?
It's of no consequence. You *can't* go wrong
If you take to heart my present ONE-WAY SONG—
Commit it to memory—at least read out loud
And memorize a goodish snatch, to shout
As you advance, looking neither to left nor right—
Never behind, nor too much to one side.
As a marching-song for One-ways it's ne plus
Ultra. Nothing can touch its martial fuss.

vii.

To go far wrong I don't see how you can,
I don't indeed, my little One-way man!
Yet, naturally, it is an artificial thing
To be the sort of *One-way* that I sing.

You can't help that. From time to time you get
That feeling that you're only half-there. Yet
What is the odds, as I remarked just now?
To be even *half-there's* not such a bad wow!
That 'gorgeous' sense of being actual
In Front, that's worth a lot. *In front* you're real.
No one can take that from you. Be a FRONT,
A bold unblushing Frontispiece—a blunt,
A plain blunt Front Man, who's no orator
As Brutus is. A jolly old front-door.
And let the devil take your hindmosts what!
A god in front, behind, a vacant lot,
A Nomansland for trashbins, a nirvana:
But on your street-front sprout a proud symbolical banana.

viii.

Revolt against these chronologic laws,
That would be madness, lunacy of course.
(What next! to go to Bedlam for your bottom,
Or have your neighbours stutter out *'he's* got 'em'!)
Swag up the Back where the bold Front should stand—
Propose to reverse the dribble of Time's sand.
It will be borne in upon you promptly how
You cannot play with Time the bull and cow,
Cannot blow hot and cold, or pick and choose,
Or toss for heads and tails—you must always lose:
You are the tail, you cannot be the head,
We *One-ways* are to *one-side* limited!—
But Back-to-the-engine travellers provide
Perhaps the paradigm for those off-side,
Or such to outwit this tide's portentous flow
Who turn their backs upon the way they go.
Were we to cast about for instances
Fool-proof to illustrate our point with these,
Why then those *Back-to-the-engine* guys afford
The best of pictures for our child's black-board.

ix.

So the *Back-to-the-engine* image is impressed!—
Are there not men convinced they are at rest
Because their breasts are where their backs should be,

Poor ostriches of Temporality!—
Occulted *backwards*, where the bird occults
Downwards his stupid head? The same results—
To be neck-deep in Nothing, abolish sight,
Is just the same whichever way you hide!
Whether you get behind your back, or sink
Beneath a horizontal covering,
That is all one: your Front is the Frontier
Of two dimensions, as it were earth and air.
The headlong flux is frontal and reverseless:
It has *direction*—the earth has *surfaces*.
Back-to-the-engine travellers are those
Who wish out of their spines to sprout a nose—
Our tri-classed life-express carries oh far more
Back-to-the-engine fares than those face-fore.
Gazing at yesterdays, they squat back-first—
Blindfolded into brand-new futures burst!
Time throws them its spent landscapes—their foreground
Is just-left places—not earth-bound but time-bound!
Back-to-the-engine travelling men are hence
The most proper wax-works to our arguments—
Appropriate dummies, stolidly to endorse
Our premises with a buffoonish force.—
And Sex, why that is of the same clay as Time—
To play both Tim and Tom is without sense or rhyme.

x.

Sex is of the same clay as Time!—of the same clay
Since both are in their essence but *One-Way*
Time is the one-way dimension: sex its tart
And subtle biological counterpart.
But even Sex is Time, too, in a sense—
That chronologic burgeoning of men's.
Is it not the sex-magnet eyeless that gives
That one-way motion to a thing that lives—
That makes us say it is alive and kicks,
Not to be classed with things, but active, full of tricks—
Which drives it on at its sex-opposite,
At rest when in contact, if it's a glove-tight-fit,
Thereby to compose that two-backed beast—give up
Its front, spherical as cup fitted to cup—

All back, as an uncut orange is all back,
The two fronts disappearing in the smack.
This kiss within the temporal universe
Is as ideal as is a point in space
However—we go full-circle never quite,
But only a relative hermaphrodite
Occurs at the intense merging of our flesh.
We are back again and sundered in a flash.
Each creature keeps his front, which is his sex,
The hollow frontage, the One-way index.
No creature but retains his vis-à-vis
Chopped-off façade, productive of Thee and Me,
Meum and tuum of the far-reaching plan
Which causes us to become man and woman.—
So Sex is of the same clay as Time—is made
Out of the same proclivities of fate.

xi.

Take next the Backs alone—take all that stares
Backwards out over the Nothing of past years—
That is a shut-book—limit—nothing else.
We are all composed half of these darkling shells—
(Since but half-minted only, since half's left
Vacant, as if to betray our sketchy weft).
What are the Backs of you and me, brother, but this
Half-finished and one-sided chrysalis?
All, there, is *That-away-from-which-man-turns*,
There all is nothing but *That-to-which-nothing-returns!*
No toes stick out to invite us to run back
There, and no eyes observe this once vivacious track:
The ships-wake of *this* ship boasts no porthole,
All that's abaft *that* beam does in pitch blackness roll!
No hands hang ready to grapple to *that* chest
A sweetheart, and no testicles ingest
Blood in a tingling bowsprit, and no nose
Scents danger or sniffs down at jasmin or rose!
No mouth gapes there, to kiss or bite you'd say:
There is no mesmeric eloquent eye-play.—
Lighted by nothing it is a mere 'Back', such as,
Reverse of his quick medal, every *One-way* has.

xii.

But the Back is father to the Front. All's young
Before. Behind from occiput to bung
All's old as is creation. Nature's face
Is accidental with the functional maze:
Not so that polished nothingness that goes
With all that lives, its hindmost end to close.
Let us praise Backs!—the Back at least is chaste—
That that can keep its place, let it be praised!
Possessing the art most tactfully to dress
Nonentity in a blank magnificentness.
Let that even above Fronts be loudly praised!
(Best to be nowt, too, than a negative thing—
So praise the reverse of what we are out to sing.)
Happy the Back that knows not its own Front,
However much unvisited, unsunned!
Oh lucky Backs that without gadgets are
Of Time's manufacture. Balistraria,
Teeth, tentacles and all the rest of it
Are left to the busy Fronts to interpret.
The biped finally's the better model
For the *perfect* Back—a blank from heel to noddle.

xiii.

I'm all for Backs then (though it is Fronts I sing)—
All for them inasmuch as frontness does spring
From this behindness, just as in mirrors all
That you perceive springs from their mercury wall—
Without that opaque backing of their glass
No reflex phantom would start out at us.—
To keep a calm sough, a peace-in-our-time pipe
Gushing a sodden cloud, the Toby-type,
Above a pot of mildly befuddling hops,
Propped up unbuttoned in the shoppiest of back-shops,
Of a nation-of-shopkeepers—with an eye to the main chance
(Not *both* eyes to it, as in closefisted France),
Where Time *is Money*, yes, but takes a nap
Sometimes, and Money even relaxes in Plenty's lap—
In a word, Old England, I'm for that every time—
Though recognizing that the once clear image is dim,
Aware, of course, that the surfaces are cracked,

A thought concave, needing badly to be rebacked,
That all the colour has left it—that it does swing,
Even, in a strange bias upward, the under-thing
Displacing the true continents of the top
(The upper thing) so that the things-of-the-Back outcrop—
Suffering a great reversal not unlike that
Of the upended cosmos (the vacant and flat
Supposed negation of the Antipodes)
Sketched by Montsurry in the first of the *Bussys*,
Her Back gnawed through with fantasies, you see
'How she is riveted with hypocrisy'!

xiv.

Be that as it may I should be sorry to be dead
From the head down, or from the front back: that head
That is in fact footless, is a factitious crown—
Summit of nothing, cut off from the neck down,
Decapitated—since what without his ship
Is a captain—the spike gone what is the tip?
What also is the briskest Front on earth
Whose Back is riveted throughout its girth—
Whose shop-front of pugnacity and pep
Is held in place with rivets in the back shop?
To be decapitated or to be *defronted*
Is much the same—from the Front backwards dead,
Or the chin downward—all that can be said
Is that the slow-footed foot suffers the less,
The spur removed, and the Back does blankly press
Onward blindbeggarly—or if it doesn't
Is none the wiser—only the Front's uncousined,
Widowed or orphaned pronto for the lack
Of a mere bagatelle—a plain unvarnished Back!

xv.

But give me England. Give me next to her
Her shadow if you have it. I think that's fair!
Give me her Back, with whatever riveted;
If her Front's in pieces, give me her Front dead!
I can't say more than that—a chip's enough
To fancy the old block-back, if it's top-carat stuff.
Give me a sort of buttercup—my loss

To shadow forth and symbolize of course.
Souvenir-hunter! rifle her corpse, but give
A pubic hair to me, with the old british whiff!
I'm for the old tart every time—for her
From Mab's queenier proto-Britannia, right back to
          Boadicea—
For Great Britain to the hilt—through thick and thin
That horsey Miss I've got under my skin.
So give me a great abstraction, when it is England—
Free-land, sea-land, the Five-o'clock land,
Tea-terminus, hop-harvest-home, sweet hospital of rum,
Borrower of Schnapps for Gin-palaces—of Crusoe and
          Kingdom-Come,
Of the cavalier fan-flirter, Party-Politics, the Lewis-gun!
But whatever else you give me, hand over or withhold!
Never give me a *sham* England!—The true Old,
The pre-victorian article, or nothing!
Nothing that has not the breezy metallic ring
As you throw it down. Never palm off a stool
Pigeon!—It must either be *all* John Bull or *no* John Bull!

xvi.

But to be *debacked*, that is the worst of the lot,
Worse than beheading. And that is what we've got.
For it is better to have a head and nothing else,
Than just the Fronts without the concomitant shells.
Our nursery of Backs, all those fate would remove—
We hang in vacuo—circle in fashion's groove.
Beyond question it is our lot to be all Front,
All temporal bustle, tantamount to a stunt
To affect to run—all the wild gestures of speed—
Stock-still in fact, we stamp out Change's seed.
(From *this* revolution there can be no revolt—
This change to all fresh change must call a halt:
Hereby we standardize the will to progress—
It is a strictly *One-way* pattern of redress.)
The trickster Time cannot perform his trick,
More than the strawless Copt could make the brick,
If he has not the dead material as well
To mix in, and ferment his temporal.
Coming from Nowhere, our advance is too ideal—

Cut off from the chief ingredient of our 'real',
The Universe of Absence—disconnect
With all that is not action—no longer reflect—
From the reserves we carry in our hump
We are parted. In consequence we *slump*.—
But all this is to be *debacked*. Backless we can
But achieve the status of the 'stuffed shirt' man.

xvii.

So much for the politics of the Fronts and Backs
(It's not our business to clobber the world's cracks)!
A sunburst of diamonds can attract our stare,
Not the extinct paste splashing the hennaed hair
Of a vaudeville empress, the mortgaged splendour hit
With death-dues, not the jazz-bred aristocrat—
That is the refuse of the pawnshop. *That*
Can be left in the gutter to hold out its hat.
As said by Flaubert, it had not the animal will
To hold what it had got—now it can only sell
Others, having long ago lost its own,
While seven-figure barons guard the Throne.
All that was once stood for by the crowned great,
Glitters in the eyeballs of the Third Estate—
We must look for leaders anywhere but in
The crapulous remnants of the 'Upper Ten'.
Under these circumstances, Citizeness,
And Citizen, let us bolster up the face
Of the debacked chaotic Time-temple of unorthodoxy.
Let us run in and instruct the unbusy bee
With a few simple dithyrambs, and *then*
Shout out a warning to all intelligent men!

xviii.

Ring all bells backwards—enter by sally-ports,
Make towers of wells, night-clubs of lunch-resorts—
Make cuirasses of feathers, walls of down—
Turn inside out the street-fronts of this town,
Till people cook and copulate on shelves
Above our thoroughfares and wash themselves
In roaring gutters in the public view—
So banish privacy, disintegrate Me and You—

Coughing on ladders tenants ascend, and those
Already up their private-parts disclose
(Lest faces vaunted a greater 'publicness'
Of spirit or of flesh, in frank undress—
Stealing a march on Mounts-of-Venuses,
Erst-codpieced aristocrats, and B.T.M.s,
And all the rest of the stuck-up *Ahems*)—
Affront no beetle by sporting bathing-drawers
Nor seem to sniff at 'man's friend' on all-fours!
So, frantically *frontal*, make an end
Once and for all of fans of the Dead-end,
The sectaries of Backness—who draw near
Given half a chance to all that is *absolute* Rear.

xix.

So let us sing the Song of the Fronts! Each day
By african bush-telegraph let us convey
Covertly the tidings of the Time-god's rebuff—
They have bubbled the world for too long with their bluff.
No more than common snuff-box chat it is
Our *rapporteur* was lulled with silver-fizz
And Lucky Strikes into a comic grin
And a condition bordering on spleen.
At the crisis of his boredom he confessed
That he worked best without his pants and vest—
And had often in the labyrinth at Antibes
Lain sun-cooked side by side with other sheep,
To make himself of Whiteness antipathic,
And meet the wishes of a kohl-lidded sapphic,
Matey and monocled.—Recovering his senses
He leapt up, circumventing their defences
He gave the Time-king tit for tat and quelled
A nude mob though his left leg had gone dead—
In spite of pins and needles put to flight
A posse of amazons, hitting out left and right.
That is the kind of nonsense to broadcast
Disseminating the successes of our counterblast.

xx.

The tongues of nineteen cantos now have smote
Upon the sodden air. I've changed my coat
As many times, you may have thought old son!
A man of fashion has more suits than one
You know, and if I come up looking different
At each fresh bout, it is always the same stiff front,
Under whatever homespun, twill or tweed,
I shroud my *one-way* sawdust-stuffed six-feet.
'Still, *who* is this Time-god or Time-king', you'll say,
'Over what if anything does he hold sway?
It's the first I've heard of His Omnipotence.
From all mention of this name the Press abstains:
Wherefore? What is against him? Is he a Nigger,
A Chink, a Jew, or some yet odder figure?
Is he spelled "Time"—does he just *sound* like that
Only, or what? He must be an acrobat
Who would dodge and duck and not be flattened out
Between the two of you, if bout by bout
One hangs around at what you call your *Song*.
Also it's none too plain to which belong
The points allotted to decide the match.
It looks as if both Time and you do scratch
The Back of t'other while you bash your Fronts,
And vice-versa. It all looks like *stunts*!'
Some such complaint would probably be heard
Either here, or later, from our One-way bird—
I know what to expect, so I have lent
My tongue to air this one-way argument.

xxi.

What value can reside in one-way things,
Again, of one who only *One-ways* sings,
I hear it asked. Let us get that over now—
Then we'll step Timewards, stiffly to kowtow.
Are we poor *One-ways* not of such a stuff
As words are wasted on? One word's enough,
Any crass epithet, to express our lot,
Of stucco Fronts, under sentence to be shot,
That strut and pant in insect packs— what's that
To agitate a serious pen? They have spat

Upon their work, the gods who thought us out.
Let us spare our pains. Fresh verse about to spout,
Poet, swallow your song—or wallow in sham!
(I get your meaning One-way). Better to slam
The door forever in the face of speech,
Confine expressive utterance to a screech?
For our *trop-plein* agree a standard scream?
Why hand down the sagas of a puppet's dream?
I'm with you—Wherefore squander pigment and ink
Upon the simulacrum of a stink?
The features of nonentity is *not*
Inspiring. A dud play with half a plot,
A one-way climax at the best—good sense
Revolts! Intellects scribble for our pence,
Dish up our half-baked spuds over again,
Half for our huzzas, half for horrid gain.
You ask—Can masterpieces the deaf-mute beguile?
To polish a bold satiric verse worth while
Might well be found if there were something there
To make it lawful to string up *Don't-Care*!
But as it is, we need no shrewd harangue
To show us that Don't-Care should *never* hang!

xxii.

And yet I find I care!—But I should not
I'm positive of that, if all were what
It looked to poor *Don't-Care* and *Should-I-Worry*.
I hurl myself through Time. The man to hurry
Am I and no mistake—why I'm all that
When neighbours cry *You'll never run to fat
The way you live!* To trap a word I'm up
At cockcrow, with a book I dine and sup,
My record of the Here and Now to fix
I burn each week a hundred midnight wicks,
Or filaments—I drive as dour a pen
As the first navigators or great mission-men.
All Time is new! You can't take that away
From even the most motheaten drab Today.
We are given a Ball to play with, and I play!
Never quite charted on account of *t*
As mathematics has it. I *feel* free—

Presented at sunrise with a novel view
(The Continent of Time being always *new*)
I find that I permit myself to rise
Betimes lest I should miss some mad surprise!
Am I not Time's man! For who else such zeal
Can show for all that chronologic 'real'—
That strange America of mere 'events'—
Dishwater-governments and new pup-tents
For bold 'explorers': Dollar-Diplomats:
Of morpho butterflies, ten-gallon hats?
Have I not marcopoloed up and down
The universe of this 'expanding' town,
Bursting with sodden nonsense? Am I not still
Tracking an unmapped landfall with my quill?
Yet who can suppose that all this wild expense
Of costly spirit, of rare commonsense,
Is a mere effect of fashionable itch
To please King Kronos or his latest bitch!

xxiii.

That never! Upon his juju I do spit—
I have torn to shreds his philosophic kit!
I've knocked the shit out of his bogus champs.
I've put out all his wreckers' lying lamps.
Yet in a sense the Time-king's fellow—a sense
There is in which I might be that: My pen's
His trusty instrument, if you by him
Should mean that imitation-timeless limb
Of Satan—then I *might* consent to join
His masquerade. If the Battle of the Boyne,
Chemin des Dames, Austerlitz, Culloden,
Were all agreed to be as good as one:
And if I were quite certain I could go
Backwards and forwards freely, express or slow,
Between New York, and Athens-when-Plato-lived—
In exchange for that I'd let the good ship drift
A bit to order. But that's *not* what's meant—
That hardly follows from the argument.
Though such a stout supporter of One-ways
I'd be none too sorry if in changing place
I could change times a little!—say *to France*

Meant *visit Montaigne*: not to countenance
Is such a pleasant tripping for those who frown
On any jaunt outside your native town—
'See your own Time first!' such conduct would call down—
From those who do, on this pretext or that,
The compass box, as restless as a rat.

xxiv.

In any medium except that of verse
Forthwith I could enlighten you. Too terse,
And as it were compact, this form of art—
Which handles the finished product only—the hard
Master-material of selected sound.
The intellect has its workshops underground;
We cannot go back, out of this dance of words,
To become the teacher. Here we behave as birds—
The brain-that-sweats *offends*, it breaks our spell,
You do see that? we really must not *smell*
In this rôle: it is aristocratic but
Cudgel your brains in this case you must *not*.
So you will understand that argument,
Except in intent stylistic, or to invent
A certain pattern, is out of the question here.
I can only release, as elegant as deer,
A herd of wandering shapes, which *may* go straight,
But are just as likely to have grandly strayed,
Before we write finis out of sight and reach.
I cannot help this. It is noblesse oblige.

xxv.

I will however, in the manner of Boileau,
The massive beams of a great searchlight throw
Upon the clouds of an impending storm,
And make the attempt to charm while I inform.—
For the time-man, then, *t* might in fact be *d*.
Should you ignore that fact, you remain at sea—
I speak of the four-dimensional quartette.
The 'motion' of old-fashioned 'matter'—get
If you can that into the socket where
You kept your mental 'time', and leave it there—
Popping 'direction' in alongside of it,

Make it a good non-concrete sort of fit.
Once that's achieved, O.K., Leibnitz allows
(I'm with the old dog there) as much as Gauss
That Time can be checked only at limited range,
Existing as a parasite on Change.
Time's not distinct from things, he thinks. Instants
Without the 'things' are legs without the pants,
Or vice-versa. Objects, when *all-at-once*,
Is 'space'. But the same is 'time'—or so it runs
In Leibnitz' text—when one-after-the-other,
You change—you move, you see—are the half-brother
Of yesterday's bonhomme, or the cousin, say,
You move—you change. And, then, you are *one-way*.—
So far so good, as far as I'm concerned,
I stand for no such absolutes—returned
Into an independent thing from change,
To me Old Gaffer Time would just look strange:
Although subscribe I do not to the thesis
That monads should be cut up into pieces,
Existent only as a myriapod.
I demand no absolute, except only God.

                                xxvi.

In my best Boileau always, I will pass
Into the clock-work labyrinths of glass,
Where etherwinds in infra-red timespaces
Impart a sickly pallor to our faces.—
Important as are powerstations, the clock
Is more so. *Esto Memor!* Sedate tick-tock!
It's my belief the Master-Clock does hold
The death-warrant of the four-faced time-manifold.
Geometry of postulates pretends
To lean on physical clocks for its own ends:
How easy though to snatch from beneath it all
That gimcrack apparatus, cause it to take a fall!
Positivism of Mach undermines in fact
Spacetimers and they get their nastiest smack,
Or will do so, from their own empirical fans—
It is *the clocks* will wind up *natura naturans*!
The infinitesimal-interval *ds*
Is their Achilles' heel, and that I bless—

I here predict their downfall, with the clock's tick
The responsible party along with the metre-stick!
On time-servers of that sort a pox I say,
Frankly I'd have those blow-flies blown away
From the mechanistic carcass, which, when it died,
The Nineteenth Century left us, and that kite
Einstein discouraged from his tricky curving,
That has proved to the highbrow riffraff so unnerving.
After ten years of making Space on earth
Endless as Time (not bludgeoned into birth
With painful fiats, in the natural fashion,
By a Creator in a fit of passion:
But sown as a cell, 'creatively', somewhere—
And *Evolution*, slow but sure, is there!)
After a decade of this temper of thinking
The very flush-box of the world has started stinking!

xxvii.

Where I join issue, as Fleet Street would say,
Is really on account of you, One-Way!
Your onewayness is threatened, that's the fact!
At least it's tampered with. You'll be debacked
If you're not very careful! And your 'will',
Why that's wiped out entirely. When you kill
Or steal or whatnot, why no 'will' precedes
The act. You hunger as a Robot feeds!
But this is very bad! It's worse than that—
They'll have you yet, or I will eat my hat!
Truffles you are to them, cheap truffles too.
I cannot think as yet what's best to do.
They've marked you down for robothood, it's no use,
You'll be the slave of a collective neo-Croesus,
Calling themselves this abstract name or that—
Chief Agent of the Proletariat—
Wherever it occurs it comes that way,
With awful *benevolence* they take up sway.
Great democrats they are, demotic tags
Sprout from their mouths, they affect in public rags
Almost, or homespun—sweatshirts and apache caps.
They are not 'One of Our Conquerors', but just 'nice chaps'!
'Your *rugged individualism* must go'!

They tell you. And they take it at one blow!
But first they teach you that you are just nix,
And wear you down with barbarous pinpricks.
The philosophy of a full-blown automaton
Is cooked up for you: and then one by one
All pleasant things removed from out your reach.
They show you hunger. Nonentity they teach.

xxviii.

But how can the mathematics of the stars
Concern the issue of class against class?
Do homo sapiens and the citizen
Affect each other in that shrewd way then—
So that to advertize as cheap as dirt
The former, must the latter's prospects hurt?
Can you drive better bargains with our sex
After dosing it with a 'little man' complex?
Can Time, a metaphysical concept,
Play any part within the marxist sept—
Time seen as 'the soul of Space'—hailed as a god—
Does that affect the average voter's lot?—
Naif and natural such query is,
For such hegemony of thought as this,
Though common to the asiatic mind,
Is foreign here, where we are less refined.
We *think* what goes on higher up the street
Or lower down will not untune *our* bleat!
Yet how a new cosmic picture might impose
Its pattern upon the gutter even—how it arose
Out of a passion of more pervasive sort
Than, proper to metre-stick or to retort,
Among pure technicians may be met with—that
Is surely not too hard to arrive at?
Ponder, how 'scientific thought', One-way,
Has changed your life for you. The Quaker may
Supply a clue—great money-men 'tis odd
To find in the same skin as men-of-god!
And metaphysics, though they play no part
In your life, *do* in protoplasm start.—
N'insistons pas! be hoodwinked if you must.
But I'll confine myself to this last thrust:

'Emergent' or 'Creative' Evolution
Has got *some* bearing on 'red' revolution.
And Time, that fleshless concept, gets a corpus
Upon the social plane, and puffs like any porpoise.
Read 'progress' for the *t* coordinate—
And for its *causal* principles read 'fate'.
And for its evolutionist drugged-tea
Read more than *impero*—read deity!

xxix.

Exclaim with me: 'Oh World, oh Life, *oh Time*!'
And make each thought with *busy body* rhyme!
Let us within the Van of Progress sit,
And make indeed a bright outing of it—
(Not crossing a single frontier, for that's lèse
Majesté, of the Majesty that stays
Himself no way at home—because he has
In fact *no* home, ubiquitous as jazz).
But all the same—a system that's at rest—
In spite of that we'll do our level best,
In pottering round our own backdoor show those
Who move more freely, that we *freely chose*
(Without any *See Britain First!* or *What's the Matter
With your Own Backyard!* or suchlike beastly chatter)
To stay at home, and 'progress' in *that* way
(Where Yogis can, we too with *self* can play,
Admire our small umbilical recess—
At least as tourists we can *dress*—and then, undress—
And make a lovely Lido of our kitchen
Just near the sink, convenient to retch in,
When we feel queasy with the rush of wind
As the ether roars about us without stint).
Then we have Time! Even if we've got no 'place'—
And is not Time in fact just mental 'space'?
We need not ever budge again from where
We first were born into a world of care.
For is not goaheadness brought *to us*,
Instead of us to it? Without any fuss
We can hear the Toulouse programme from the pub—
In our time-cosmos everywhere's the hub!

It is unmodern, and expensive, too,
To move about,—in our *own* fat we stew!

xxx.

Therefore: 'The course is timewards'! I exclaim.
'Timewards she is!' you echo. Spanish Main
Of our time-travel promises no gold,
What matter though? Mercurial and bold
We find a New Land, a lost Lyonesse
At every breathless daybreak, more or less.
With trowel and vasculum we swiftly land,
Theodolites cut up the mystery-strand:
Then pulling up the hook, we speed away,
Shooting the sun (and stars) as best we may:
Log-glass and line inform us of our pace,
And so, drunk with the New, we gladly race
Upon fresh spectacles, risen overnight,
The fortresses of spice, great baths of light.
We figure by dead reckoning we go true,
And true we go, we never want for 'the new'.
Strange shores shoot up-and-down, some brown, some
      pink,
It depends on the convulsion, and then sink—
As it is said that Rapa Nui does
And many one-day archipelagos.
Who is the captain of this happy scow?
It's *me*, you get me, is the skipper now!
Writing by binnacle-lamplight I make out
The log—in the matter of landfalls do us proud.
No matter if the next ship looks in vain
For these short-lived time-islands of our Main,
Our temporal Pacific! One, two, three!
We spot fresh atolls between lunch and tea.
And in the sunset pearlinglugger fleets
Betray the presence of still further treats
For pop-eyed look-outs, and kanaka lands
Come up between the watches with their sands.
Reversed lagoons, for our unsceptic eye,
Show (inside-out) how the new land does lie!

xxxi.

Chapultepec Park is a fashion of Versailles.
Mexico City, seen by an aztec eye,
Would be a chimera, only geographically grafted
Upon the solid past, unstably if stolidly draughted—
Otherwise as off the map as a ring of Saturn,
If not more so, in its incongruous pattern.
Similarly a flight of Fokkers, Vickers and Spads
Would have looked caddish (built for us wingless cads)
To a frigate-bird above Columbus' poop,
Or one shadowing Pizarro's pirate sloop
Off Tumbez, hurrying to investigate
The Inca's prodigality of plate.
These are the Time King's doings. The Time God's—
For king's no adequate title! He replots
With an itch for a silly novelty you may say
All the bricks and mortar that should come his way—
With his odd geometries, from the saxon field
To the american city, beblocked, beglassed, besteeled.
A sort of scratching upon an obsidian block
No more, a mixing of this and of that stock,
All of which he never could have *invented*—
He's a mixer and shaker at most—he's only rented
A ball of stone on which to scratch his patterns,
And six big ponds upon whose fish he battens—
And an excellent 'shooting' in some thick patches of forest—
And set himself up as Butcher, Graver and Florist!

xxxii.

Gone with his dogsrib now is the penny-shocker—
He is only a house breaking half-wit, an unlocker
By skeleton keys. Of the 'New' a spirited faker—
Which is no better than an 'antique' shammer and crack-
         maker!
No builder he, but can think up a concoction—
Polish a scrapheap, bought at a bankrupt-auction.
Follow a blind engineer—with clapboard and glass,
Tinfoil and sheetiron, vamp up an architect's farce!
A spoiler, with patchwork devices, such he has been
Since first, a slick understudy, he came on the scene.
Such version is *Time* up-to-date—I patent it here.

An abstraction called 'Father', but now, year by year,
Younger and brighter, matching our Nancies at that—
No scythe or the rest of it—curls in the place of a hat,
A sweatshirt bespeaking prowess, a skin-diver's suit,
Bar the bags and vest, a sandalled Mercury-boot—
An airman what! (*Time flies!*) and yes, a great air
Of being just Nobody, and at the same time *Don't-Care*!
He's a thought bloodshot's had rotten Klieg-eye:
Since he's so youthful, he's praps a thought *too* shy.
A pensile lock, it's forever jolted back,
A suburban hiker's military pack.
Such, if you meet him's Time—but don't look for eld:
Each day Time's born again, with a brand-new pelt.

xxxiii.

Ah well, my One-way, there you have my song.
I cannot now this argument prolong.
I have a date with another book—Next week
I am due upon *One-way* complaints to speak—
What the One-Way must guard against *as such*—
Pathology of Fronts—Why use a crutch?
Problems of equilibrium for those
Who go upright, and follow their own nose;
Care of the sick, who front-ways-up repose.
Treatment for maladies of the bust and belly,
And how to act from Sundown to revelly—
A strictly progressive *one-way* slumber-chart—
Avoidance of dreams—the horse before the cart
To keep, *in spite of* the quadruped—What books
For the One-way bookcase. I think that looks
A busy timetable, I'm pressed you see.
Excuse me from all further advocacy
Of strict observance of a one-way type
Of thinking and behaving. Keep your pipe
Well to the fore gripped in mock-mastiff jaws
And put your best foot foremost too of course.
But above all my parting shot is this—
Your *best* interests are served if you dismiss
In their *totality* inquisitive thoughts—
Bearing upon biology. Those sorts
Of questions you may leave to introspectors,

Who are not men, but psychical inspectors—
They will make you most self-conscious if you heed them.
Keep your wits dull on purpose: you don't need them!
A man's a man for a' that—never forget
Your doctor's only another kind of Vet.

ENVOI

If I have not trod the romantic path, blame me!
If it has been a man singing and not a bird—
If so the bird you be to curse, curse me
Poor Parrot! Then I will teach you *another* word!
If plain speech brings the blush beneath the dirt
I'm sorry if you hate the thing you heard—
But I meant that you should get it, classic and clear,
Between the eyes, or in the centre of the ear!
As plain as the 'Burgess-gentleman' got his
In natural verses, or the 'Ridiculous Miss',
These times require a tongue that naked goes,
Without more fuss than Dryden's or Defoe's.

The Bailiff billed in Number One 'Fight-talk'
Was a curtain-raiser, to last a minute or two.
Song Two was a sketch of a critical cake-walk.
The romantic standpoint (a good standpoint too).
Song three was Me—the electric-hare that's Me—
A Me that blots out for the moment You.
Song Four was the lament of *Not-to-be*,
Conveying that the Me alone is true!

Then what I've done, of that I know I've done,
Is to provide the pattern of a stave
To be the folk-song of your Number One,
Deep as the Many's and a good deal more brave.

ENEMY OF THE STARS

Synopsis in **PROGRAMME.**

ADVERTISEMENT

THE SCENE. | SOME BLEAK CIRCUS, UNCOVERED, CAREFULLY-CHOSEN, VIVID NIGHT. IT IS PACKED WITH POSTERITY, SILENT AND EXPECTANT. POSTERITY IS SILENT, LIKE THE DEAD, AND MORE PATHETIC.

CHARACTERS.

TWO HEATHEN CLOWNS, GRAVE BOOTH ANIMALS

CYNICAL ATHLETES.

DRESS. ENORMOUS YOUNGSTERS, BURSTING EVERY-WHERE THROUGH HEAVY TIGHT CLOTHES, LABOURED IN BY DULL EXPLOSIVE MUSCLES, full of fiery dust and sinewy energetic air, not sap. BLACK CLOTH CUT SOMEWHERE, NOWADAYS, ON THE UPPER BALTIC.

VERY WELL ACTED BY YOU AND ME.

ONE IS IN IMMENSE COLLAPSE OF CHRONIC PHILO-
SOPHY. YET HE BULGES ALL OVER, COMPLEX FRUIT,
WITH SIMPLE FIRE OF LIFE. GREAT MASK, VENUSTIC
AND VERIDIC, TYPE OF FEMININE BEAUTY CALLED
'MANNISH'.

FIRST HE IS ALONE. A HUMAN BULL RUSHES INTO
THE CIRCUS. THIS SUPER IS NO MORE IMPORTANT
THAN LOUNGING STAR OVERHEAD. HE IS NOT EVEN A
'STAR'. HE RUSHES OFF, INTO THE EARTH.

CHARACTERS AND PROPERTIES BOTH EMERGE
FROM GANGWAY INTO GROUND AT ONE SIDE.

THEN AGAIN THE PROTAGONIST REMAINS NEGLEC-
TED, AS THOUGH HIS TWO FELLOW ACTORS HAD FOR-
GOTTEN HIM, CAROUSING IN THEIR PROFESSIONAL
CAVERN.

SECOND CHARACTER, APPALLING 'GAMIN,' BLACK
BOURGEOIS ASPIRATIONS UNDERMINING BLATANT
VIRTUOSITY OF SELF.

His criminal instinct of intemperate bilious heart, put at
service of unknown Humanity, our King, to express its violent
royal aversion to Protagonist, statue-mirage of Liberty in the
great desert.

Mask of discontent, anxious to explode, restrained by qualms
of vanity, and professional coyness. Eyes grown venturesome
in native temperatures of Pole—indulgent and familiar, blessing
with white nights.

Type of characters taken from broad faces where Europe
grows arctic, intense, human and universal.

'Yet you and me: why not from the English metropolis?'—
Listen: it is our honeymoon. We go abroad for the first scene
of our drama. Such a strange thing as our coming together
requires a strange place for initial stages of our intimate
ceremonious acquaintance.

THERE ARE TWO SCENES

STAGE ARRANGEMENTS.

RED OF STAINED COPPER PREDOMINANT COLOUR. OVERTURNED CASES AND OTHER IMPEDIMENTA HAVE BEEN COVERED, THROUGHOUT ARENA, WITH OLD SAIL-CANVAS.

HUT OF SECOND SCENE IS SUGGESTED BY CHARACTERS TAKING UP THEIR POSITION AT OPENING OF SHAFT LEADING DOWN INTO MIMES' QUARTERS.

A GUST, SUCH AS IS MET IN THE CORRIDORS OF THE TUBE, MAKES THEIR CLOTHES SHIVER OR FLAP, AND BLARES UP THEIR VOICES. MASKS FITTED WITH TRUMPETS OF ANTIQUE THEATRE, WITH EFFECT OF TWO CHILDREN BLOWING AT EACH OTHER WITH TIN TRUMPETS.

AUDIENCE LOOKS DOWN INTO SCENE, AS THOUGH IT WERE A HUT ROLLED HALF ON ITS BACK, DOOR UPWARDS, CHARACTERS GIDDILY MOUNTING IN ITS OPENING.

THE PLAY

ARGHOL

INVESTMENT OF RED UNIVERSE.
EACH FORCE ATTEMPTS TO SHAKE HIM.
CENTRAL AS STONE, POISED MAGNET OF SUBTLE, VAST, SELFISH THINGS.
HE LIES LIKE HUMAN STRATA OF INFERNAL BIOLOGIES. WALKS LIKE WARY SHIFTING OF BODIES IN DISTANT EQUIPOISE. SITS LIKE A GOD BUILT BY AN ARCHITECTURAL STREAM, FECUNDED BY MAD BLASTS OF SUNLIGHT.

———

The first stars appear and Arghol comes out of the hut. This is his cue. The stars are his cast. He is rather late and snips into its place a vest button. A noise falls on the cream of Posterity, assembled in silent banks. One hears the gnats' song of the thirtieth centuries.

They strain to see him, a gladiator who has come to fight a ghost, Humanity—the great Sport of Future Mankind.

He is the prime athlete exponent of this sport in its palmy days. Posterity slowly sinks into the hypnotic trance of Art, and the Arena is transformed into the necessary scene.

THE RED WALLS OF THE UNIVERSE NOW SHUT THEM IN, WITH THIS CONDEMNED PROTAGONIST.

THEY BREATHE IN CLOSE ATMOSPHERE OF TERROR AND NECESSITY TILL THE EXECUTION IS OVER, THE RED WALLS RECEDE, THE UNIVERSE SATISFIED.

THE BOX OFFICE RECEIPTS HAVE BEEN ENORMOUS.

———

THE ACTION OPENS

THE YARD

The Earth has burst, a granite flower, and disclosed the scene. A wheelwright's yard.

Full of dry, white volcanic light.

Full of emblems of one trade: stacks of pine, iron, wheels stranded.

Rough Eden of one soul, to whom another man, and not Eve, would be mated.

A canal at one side, the night pouring into it like blood from a butcher's pail.

Rouge mask in aluminum mirror, sunset's grimace through the night.

A leaden gob, slipped at zenith, first drop of violent night, spreads cataclysmically in harsh water of evening. Caustic Reckitt's stain.

Three trees, above canal, sentimental, black and conventional in number, drive leaf flocks, with jeering cry.

Or they slightly bend their joints, impassible acrobats; step rapidly forward, faintly incline their heads.

Across the mud in pond of the canal their shadows are gawky toy crocodiles, sawed up and down by infant giant?

Gollywog of arabian symmetry, several tons, Arghol drags them in blank nervous hatred.

THE SUPER.

Arghol crosses yard to the banks of the canal: sits down.
'Arghol!'
'I am here.'
His voice raucous and disfigured with a catarrh of lies in the fetid bankrupt atmosphere of life's swamp: clear and splendid among Truth's balsamic hills, shepherding his agile thoughts.
'Arghol!'
It was like a child's voice hunting its mother.
A note of primitive distress edged the thick bellow. The figure rushed without running. Arghol heeled over to the left. A boot battered his right hand ribs. These were the least damaged: it was their turn.
Upper lip shot down, half covering chin, his body reached methodically. At each blow, in muscular spasm, he made the pain pass out. Rolled and jumped, crouched and flung his grovelling Enceladus weight against it, like swimmer with wave.
The boot, and heavy shadow above it, went. The self-centred and elemental shadow, with whistling noise peculiar to it, passed softly and sickly into a doorway's brown light.
The second attack, pain left by first shadow, lashing him, was worse. He lost consciousness.

THE NIGHT

His eyes woke first, shaken by rough moonbeams. A white, crude volume of brutal light blazed over him. Immense bleak electric advertisement of God, it crushed with wild emptiness of stress.
The ice field of the sky swept and crashed silently. Blowing wild organism into the hard splendid clouds, some will cast its glare, as well, over him.
The canal ran in one direction, his blood, weakly, in the opposite.

The stars shone madly in the archaic blank wilderness of the universe, machines of prey.

Mastodons, placid in electric atmosphere, white rivers of power. They stood in eternal black sunlight.

Tigers are beautiful imperfect brutes.

Throats iron eternities, drinking heavy radiance, limbs towers of blatant light, the stars poised, immensely distant, with their metal sides, pantheistic machines.

The farther, the more violent and vivid, Nature: weakness crushed out of creation! Hard weakness, a flea's size, pinched to death in a second, could it get so far.

He rose before this cliff of cadaverous beaming force, imprisoned in a messed socket of existence.

Will Energy some day reach Earth like violent civilization, smashing or hardening all? In his mind a chip of distant hardness, tugged at dully like a tooth, made him ache from top to toe.

But the violences of all things had left him so far intact.

HANP

I.

Hanp comes out of hut, coughing like a goat, rolling a cigarette. He goes to where Arghol is lying. He stirs him with his foot roughly.

Arghol strains and stretches elegantly, face over shoulder, like a woman.

'Come, you fool, and have supper.' Hanp walks back to hut, leaving him.

Arghol lies, hands clasped round his knees. This new kick has put him into a childish lethargy. He gets to his feet soon, and walks to hut. He puts his hand on Hanp's shoulder, who has been watching him, and kisses him on the cheek.

Hanp shakes him off with fury and passes inside hut.

Bastard violence of his half-disciple, métis of an apache of the icy steppe, sleek citizen, and his own dumbfounding soul.

Fungi of sullen violent thoughts, investing primitive vegetation. Hot words drummed on his ear every evening: abuse: question. Groping hands strummed toppling Byzantine organ of his mind, producing monotonous black fugue.

Harsh bayadère-shepherdess of Pamir, with her Chinese beauty: living on from month to month in utmost tent with wastrel, lean as mandrake root, red and precocious: with heavy black odour of vast Manchurian garden-deserts, and the disreputable muddy gold squandered by the unknown sun of the Amur.

His mind unlocked, free to this violent hand. It was his mind's one cold flirtation, then cold love. Excelling in beauty, marked out for Hindu fate of sovereign prostitution, but clear of the world, with furious vow not to return. The deep female strain succumbed to this ragged spirt of crude manhood, masculine with blunt wilfulness and hideous stupidity of the fecund horde of men, phallic wand-like cataract incessantly poured into God. This pip of icy spray struck him on the mouth. He tasted it with new pleasure, before spitting it out: acrid.

To be spat back among men. The young man foresaw the event.

They ate their supper at the door of the hut. An hour passed in wandering spacious silence.

'Was it bad tonight?' a fierce and railing question often repeated.

Arghol lay silent, his hands a thick shell fitting back of head, his face grey vegetable cave.

'Can't you kill him, in the name of God? A man has his hands, little else. Mote and speck, the universe illimitable!' Hanp gibed. 'It is true he is a speck, but all men are. To you he is immense.'

They sat, two grubby shadows, unvaccinated as yet by the moon's lymph, sickened by the immense vague infections of night.

'That is absurd. I have explained to you. Here I get routine, the will of the universe manifested with directness and persistence. Figures of persecution are accidents or adventures for some. Prick the thin near heart, like a pea, and the bubble puffs out. That would not be of the faintest use in my case.'

Two small black flames, wavering, as their tongues moved, drumming out thought, with low earth-draughts and hard sudden winds dropped like slapping birds from climaxes in the clouds.

No Morris-lens would have dragged them from the key of

vastness. They must be severe midgets, brain specks of the vertiginous, seismic, vertebrate, slowly-living lines, of landscape.

'Self, sacred act of violence, is like murder on my face and hands. The stain won't come out. It is the one piece of property all communities have agreed it is illegal to possess. The sweetest-tempered person, once he discovers you are that sort of criminal, changes any opinion of you, and is on his guard. When mankind cannot overcome a personality, it has an immemorial way out of the difficulty. It becomes it. It imitates and assimilates that Ego until it is no longer one. . . . This is success.

Between Personality and Mankind it is always a question of dog and cat; they are diametrically opposed species. Self is the ancient race, the rest are the new one. Self is the race that lost. But Mankind still suspects Egotistic plots, and hunts Pretenders.

My uncle is very little of a relation. It would be foolish to kill him. He is an échantillon, acid advertisement slipped in letter-box: space's store-rooms dense with frivolous originals. I am used to him, as well.'

Arghol's voice had no modulations of argument. Weak now, it handled words numbly, like tired compositor. His body was quite strong again and vivacious. Words acted on it as rain on a plant. It got a stormy neat brilliance in this soft shower. One flame balanced giddily erect, while other larger one swerved and sang with speech coldly before it.

They lay in a pool of bleak brown shadow, disturbed once by a rat's plunging head. It seemed to rattle along, yet slide on oiled planes. Arghol shifted his legs mechanically. It was a hutch with low loft where they slept.

Beyond the canal, brute-lands, shuttered with stoney clouds, lay in heavy angles of sand. They were squirted on by twenty ragged streams; legions of quails hopped parasitically in the miniature cliffs.

Arghol's uncle was a wheelwright on the edge of the town.

Two hundred miles to north the Arctic circle swept. Sinister tramps, its winds came wandering down the high road, fatigued and chill, doors shut against them.

'First of all; lily pollen of Ideal on red badge of your predatory category. Scrape this off and you lose your appetite. Obviously.—But I don't want in any case to eat Smith, because he is tough and distasteful to me. I am too vain to do harm, too superb ever to lift a finger when harmed.

A man eats his mutton chop, forgetting it is his neighbour; drinks every evening blood of the Christs, and gossips of glory.

Existence; loud feeble sunset, blaring like lumpish, savage clown, alive with rigid tinsel, before a misty door: announcing events, tricks and a thousand follies, to penniless herds, their eyes red with stupidity.

To leave violently slow monotonous life is to take header into the boiling starry cold. (For with me some guilty fire of friction unspent in solitariness, will reach the stars.)

Hell of those Heavens uncovered, whirling pit, every evening! You cling to any object, dig your nails in earth, not to drop into it.'

The night plunged gleaming nervous arms down into the wood, to wrench it up by the roots. Restless and rhythmical, beyond the staring red rimmed doorway, giddy and expanding in drunken walls, its heavy drastic lights shifted.

Arghol could see only ponderous arabesques of red cloud, whose lines did not stop at door's frame, but pressed on into shadows within the hut, in tyrannous continuity. As a cloud drove eastward, out of this frame, its weight passed, with spiritual menace, into the hut. A thunderous atmosphere thickened above their heads.

Arghol, paler, tossed clumsily and swiftly from side to side, as though asleep.

He got nearer the door. The clouds had room to waste themselves. The land continued in dull form, one per cent. animal, these immense bird-amoebas. Nerves made the earth pulse up against his side and reverberate. He dragged hot palms along the ground, caressing its explosive harshness.

All merely exterior attack.

His face calm seismograph of eruptions in Heaven.

Head of black, eagerly carved, herculean Venus, of iron tribe, hyper barbarous and ascetic. Lofty tents, sonorous with October rains, swarming from vast bright doll-like Asiatic lakes.

Faces following stars in blue rivers, till sea-struck, thundering engine of red water.

Pink idle brotherhood of little stars, passed over by rough cloud of sea.

Cataclysm of premature decadence.

Extermination of the resounding, sombre, summer tents in a decade, furious mass of images left: no human.

Immense production of barren muscular girl idols, wood verdigris, copper, dull paints, flowers.

Hundred idols to a man, and a race swamped in hurricane of art, falling on big narrow souls of its artists.

Head heavy and bird-like, weighted to strike, living on his body, ungainly red Atlantic wave.

'To have read all the books of the town, Arghol, and to come back here to take up this life again.'

Coaxing: genuine stupefaction: reproach, a trap.

Arghol once more preceded him through his soul, unbenevolent. Doors opened on noisy blankness, coming through from calm, reeling noon-loudness beyond. Garrets waking like faces. A shout down a passage to show its depth, horizon as well. Voice coming back with suddenness of expert pugilistics.

Perpetual inspector of himself.

'I must live, like a tree, where I grow. An inch to left or right would be too much.

In the town I felt unrighteous in escaping blows, home anger, destiny of here.

Selfishness, flouting of destiny, to step so much as an inch out of the bull's eye of your birth. (When it is obviously a bull's eye!)

A visionary tree, not migratory: visions from within.

A man with headache lies in deliberate leaden inanimation. He isolates his body, floods it with phlegm, sucks numbness up to his brain.

A soul wettest dough, doughiest lead: a bullet. To drop down Eternity like a plummet.

Accumulate in myself, day after day, dense concentration of pig life. Nothing spent, stored rather in strong stagnation, till rid at last of evaporation and lightness characteristic of men. So burst Death's membrane through, slog beyond, not float in appalling distances.

Energy has been fixed on me from nowhere—heavy and astonished: resigned. Or is it for remote sin! I will use it, anyway, as prisoner his bowl or sheet for escape: not as means of idle humiliation.

One night Death left his card. I was not familiar with the name he chose: but the black edge was deep. I flung it back. A thousand awakenings of violence.

Next day I had my knife up my sleeve as my uncle came at

me, ready for what you recommend. But a superstition, habit, is there, curbing him mathematically: that of not killing me. I should know an ounce of effort more.—He loads my plate, even. He must have palpable reasons for my being alive.'

————

A superb urchin watching some centre of angry commotion in the street, his companion kept his puffed slit eyes, generously cruel, fixed on him. God and Fate, constant protagonists, one equivalent to Police, his simple sensationalism was always focussed on. But God was really his champion. He longed to see God fall on Arghol, and wipe the earth with him. He egged God on: then egged on Arghol. His soft rigid face grinned with intensity of attention, propped contemplatively on hand.

Port-prowler, serf of the capital, serving its tongue and gait within the grasp and aroma of the white, matt, immense sea. Abstract instinct of sullen seafarer, dry-salted in slow acrid airs, aerian flood not stopped by shore, dying in dirty warmth of harbour-boulevards.

His soul like ocean-town: leant on by two skies. Lower opaque one washes it with noisy clouds: or lies giddily flush with street crevices, wedges of black air, flooding it with red emptiness of dead light.

It sends ships between its unchanging slight rock of houses periodically, slowly to spacious centre. Nineteen big ships, like nineteen nomad souls for its amphibious sluggish body, locked there.

II.

'What is destiny? Why yours to stay here, more than to live in the town or cross to America?'

'My dear Hanp, your geography is so up-to-date!

Geography doesn't interest me. America is geography.

I've explained to you what the town is like.

Offences against the discipline of the universe are registered by a sort of conscience, prior to the kicks. Blows rain on me. Mine is not a popular post. It is my destiny right enough: an extremely unpleasant one.'

'It is not the destiny of a man like you to live buried in this cursed hole.'

'Our soul is wild, with primitiveness of its own. Its wilderness is anywhere—in a shop, sailing, reading psalms: its greatest good our destiny.

Anything I possess is drunk up here on the world's brink, by big stars, and returned me in the shape of thought heavy as a meteorite. The stone of the stars will do for my seal and emblem. I practise with it, monotonous "putting," that I may hit Death when he comes.'

'Your thought is buried in yourself.'

'A thought weighs less in a million brains than in one. No one is conjuror enough to prevent spilling. Rather the bastard form infects the original. Famous men are those who have exchanged themselves against a thousand idiots. When you hear a famous man has died penniless and diseased, you say, "Well served." Part of life's arrangement is that the few best become these cheap scarecrows.

The process and condition of life, without any exception, is a grotesque degradation, and "souillure" of the original solitude of the soul. There is no help for it, since each gesture and word partakes of it, and the child has already covered himself with mire.

Anything but yourself is dirt. Anybody that is. I do not feel clean enough to die, or to make it worth while killing myself.'

———

A laugh, packed with hatred, not hoping to carry, snapped like a fiddle-cord.

'Sour grapes! That's what it's all about! And you let yourself be kicked to death here out of spite.

Why do you talk to me, I should like to know? Answer me that?'

Disrespect or mocking is followed, in spiritualistic séances, with offended silence on part of the spooks. Such silence, not discernedly offended, now followed.

The pseudo-rustic Master, cavernously, hemicyclically real, but anomalous shamness on him in these circumstances, poudre de riz on face of knight's sleeping effigy, lay back indifferent, his feet lying, two heavy closed books, before the disciple.

Arghol was a large open book, full of truths and insults.

He opened his jaws wide once more in egotistic self castigation.

'The doctoring is often fouler than disease.

Men have a loathsome deformity called Self: affliction got through indiscriminate rubbing against their fellows: social excrescence.

Their being is regulated by exigencies of this affliction. Only one operation can cure it: the suicide's knife.

Or an immense snuffling or taciturn parasite, become necessary to victim, like abortive poodle, all nerves, vice and dissatisfaction.

I have smashed it against me, but it still writhes, turbulent mess.

I have shrunk it in frosty climates, but it has filtered filth inward through me, dispersed till my deepest solitude is impure.

Mire stirred up desperately, without success in subsequent hygiene.'

This focussed disciple's physical repulsion: nausea of humility added. Perfect tyrannic contempt: but choking respect, curiosity; consciousness of defeat. These two extremes clashed furiously. The contempt claimed its security and triumph: the other sentiment baffled it. His hatred of Arghol for perpetually producing this second sentiment grew. This would have been faint without physical repulsion to fascinate him, make him murderous and sick.

He was strong and insolent with consciousness stuffed in him in anonymous form of vastness of Humanity: full of rage at gigantic insolence and superiority, combined with utter uncleanness and despicableness—all back to physical parallel—of his Master.

The more Arghol made him realize his congenital fatuity and cheapness, the more a contemptible matter appeared accumulated in the image of his Master, sunken mirror. The price of this sharp vision of mastery was contamination.

Too many things inhabited together in this spirit for cleanliness or health. Is one soul too narrow an abode for genius?

To have humanity inside you—to keep a doss-house! At least impossible to organize on such a scale.

People are right who would disperse these impure monopolies! Let everyone get his little bit, intellectual Balham rather than Bedlam!

III.

In sluggish but resolute progress towards the City and centre, on part of young man was to be found cause of Arghol's ascendancy in first place. Arghol had returned some months only from the great city of their world.

He showed Hanp picture postcards. He described the character of each scene. Then he had begun describing more closely. At length, systematically he lived again there for his questioner, exhausted the capital, put it completely in his hands. The young man had got there without going there. But instead of satisfying him, this developed a wild desire to start off at once. Then Arghol said:—

'Wait a moment.'

He whispered something in his ear.

'Is that true?'

'Aye and more.'

He supplemented his description with a whole life of comment and disillusion.—The young man felt now that he had left the city. His life was being lived for him.—But he forgot this and fought for his first city. Then he began taking a pleasure in destruction.

He had got under Arghol's touch.

But when he came to look squarely at his new possession, which he had exchanged for his city, he found it wild, incredibly sad, hateful stuff.

Somehow, however, the City had settled down in Arghol. He must seek it there, and rescue it from that tyrannic abode. He could not now start off without taking this unreal image city with him. He sat down to invest it, Arghol its walls.

IV.

Arghol had fallen. His Thébaide had been his Waterloo. He now sat up slowly.

'Why do I speak to you?

It's not to you but myself.—I think it's a physical matter: simply to use one's mouth.

My thoughts to walk abroad and not always be stuffed up in my head: ideas to banjo this resounding body.

You seemed such a contemptible sort of fellow that there was some hope for you. Or to be clear, there was NOTHING to hope from your vile character.

That is better than little painful somethings!

I am amazed to find that you are like me.

I talk to you for an hour and get more disgusted with myself.

I find I wanted to make a naif yapping Poodle-parasite of you.—I shall always be a prostitute.

I wanted to make you my self: you understand?

Every man who wants to make another HIMSELF, is seeking a companion for his detached ailment of a self.

You are an unclean little beast, crept gloomily out of my ego. You are the world, brother, with its family objections to me.

Go back to our Mother and spit in her face for me!

I wish to see you no more here! Leave at once. Here is money. Take train at once: Berlin is the place for your pestilential little carcass. Get out! Here! Go!'

Amazement had stretched the disciple's face back like a mouth, then slowly it contracted, the eyes growing smaller, chin more prominent, old and clenched like a fist.

Arghol's voice rang coldly in the hut, a bell beaten by words.

Only the words, not tune of bell, had grown harder. At last they beat virulently.

When he had finished, silence fell like guillotine between them, severing bonds.

———

The disciple spoke with his own voice, which he had not used for some weeks. It sounded fresh, brisk and strange to him, half live garish salt fish.

His mouth felt different.

'Is that all?'

Arghol was relieved at sound of Hanp's voice, no longer borrowed, and felt better disposed towards him. The strain of this mock life, or real life, rather, was tremendous on his underworld of energy and rebellious muscles. This cold outburst was not commensurate with it. It was twitch of loud bound nerve only.

'Bloody glib-tongued cow! You think you can treat me that way!'

Hanp sprang out of the ground, a handful of furious movements: flung himself on Arghol.

———

Once more the stars had come down.
Arghol used his fists.
To break vows and spoil continuity of instinctive behaviour,
lose a prize that would only be a trophy tankard never drunk
from, is always fine.
Arghol would have flung away his hoarding and scraping
of thought as well now. But his calm, long instrument of
thought, was too heavy. It weighed him down, resisted his
swift anarchist effort, and made him giddy.
His fear of death, anti-manhood, words coming out of
caverns of belief—synthesis, that is, of ideal life—appalled him
with his own strength.
Strike his disciple as he had abused him. Suddenly give way.
Incurable self taught you a heroism.
The young man brought his own disgust back to him. Full
of disgust: therefore disgusting. He felt himself on him. What
a cause of downfall!

V.

The great beer-coloured sky, at the fuss, leapt in fête of
green gaiety.
Its immense lines bent like whalebones and sprang back
with slight deaf thunder.
The sky, two clouds, their two furious shadows, fought.
The bleak misty hospital of the horizon grew pale with fluid
of anger.
The trees were wiped out in a blow.
The hut became a new boat inebriated with electric milky
human passion, poured in.
It shrank and struck them: struck, in its course, in a stirred
up unmixed world, by tree, or house-side grown wave.
First they hit each other, both with blows about equal in
force—on face and head.
Soul perched like aviator in basin of skull, more alert and
smaller than on any other occasion. Mask stoic with energy:

thought cleaned off slick—pure and clean with action. Bodies grown brain, black octopi.

Flushes on silk epiderm and fierce card-play of fists between: emptying of 'hand' on soft flesh-table.

Arms of grey windmills, grinding anger on stone of the new heart.

Messages from one to another, dropped down anywhere when nobody is looking, reaching brain by telegraph: most desolating and alarming messages possible.

The attacker rushed in drunk with blows. They rolled, swift jagged rut, into one corner of shed: large insect scuttling roughly to hiding.

Stopped astonished.

Fisticuffs again: then rolled kicking air and each other, springs broken, torn from engine.

Hanp's punch wore itself out, soon, on herculean clouds, at mad rudder of boat on Arghol.

Then like a punch-ball, something vague and swift struck him on face, exhausted and white.

Arghol did not hit hard. Like something inanimate, only striking as rebound and as attacked.

He became soft, blunt paw of Nature, taken back to her bosom, mechanically; slowly and idly winning.

He became part of responsive landscape: his friend's active punch key of the commotion.

Hanp fell somewhere in the shadow: there lay.

Arghol stood rigid.

As the nervous geometry of the world in sight relaxed, and went on with its perpetual mystic invention, he threw himself down where he had been lying before.

A strong flood of thought passed up to his fatigued head, and at once dazed him. Not his body only, but being was out of training for action: puffed and exhilarated. Thoughts fell on it like punches.

His mind, baying mastiff, he flung off.

In steep struggle he rolled into sleep.

Two clear thoughts had intervened between fight and sleep.

Now a dream began valuing, with its tentative symbols, preceding events.

———

A black jacket and shirt hung on nails across window: a gas jet turned low to keep room warm, through the night, sallow chill illumination: dirty pillows, black and thin in middle, worn down by rough head, but congested at each end.

Bedclothes crawling over bed never-made, like stagnant waves and eddies to be crept beneath.—Picture above pillow of Rosa Bonheur horses trampling up wall like well fed toffyish insects. Books piled on table and chair, open at some page.

Two texts in Finnish. Pipes half smoked, collars: past days not effaced beneath perpetual tidiness, but scraps and souvenirs of their accidents lying in heaps.

His room in the city, nine feet by six, grave big enough for the six corpses that is each living man.

Appalling tabernacle of Self and Unbelief.

He was furious with this room, tore down jacket and shirt, and threw the window open.

The air made him giddy.

He began putting things straight.

The third book, stalely open, which he took up to shut, was the 'Einzige und Sein Eigentum'.

Stirner.

One of seven arrows in his martyr mind.

Poof! he flung it out of the window.

A few minutes, and there was a knock at his door. It was a young man he had known in the town, but now saw for the first time, seemingly. He had come to bring him the book, fallen into the roadway.

'I thought I told you to go!' he said.

The young man had changed into his present disciple.

Obliquely, though he appeared now to be addressing Stirner.

'I thought I told you to go!'

His visitor changed a third time.

A middle aged man, red cropped head and dark eyes, self-possessed, loose, free, student-sailor, fingering the book: coming to a decision. Stirner as he had imagined him.

'Get out, I say. Here is money.'

Was the money for the book?

The man flung it at his head; its cover slapped him sharply.

'Glib tongued cow! Take that!'

A scrap ensued, physical experiences of recent fight recurring, ending in eviction of this visitor, and slamming of door.

'These books are all parasites. Poodles of the mind, Chows and King Charles; eternal prostitute.

The mind, perverse and gorgeous.

All this Art life, posterity and the rest, is wrong. Begin with these.'

He tore up his books.

A pile by door ready to sweep out.

He left the room, and went round to Café to find his friends.

'All companions of parasite Self. No single one a brother.

My dealings with these men is with their parasite composite selves, not with Them.'

The night had come on suddenly. Stars like clear rain soaked chillily into him.

No one was in the street.

The sickly houses oozed sad human electricity.

He had wished to clean up, spiritually, his room, obliterate or turn into deliberate refuse, accumulations of Self.

Now a similar purging must be undertaken among his companions preparatory to leaving the city.

But he never reached the Café.

His dream changed; he was walking down the street in his native town, where he now was, and where he knew no one but his school-mates, workmen, clerks in export of hemp, grain and wood.

Ahead of him he saw one of the friends of his years of study in Capital.

He did not question how he had got there, but caught him up. Although brusquely pitched elsewhere, he went on with his plan.

'Sir, I wish to know you!'

Provisional smile on face of friend, puzzled.

'Hallo, Arghol, you seem upset.'

'I wish to make your acquaintance.'

'But, my dear Arghol, what's the matter with you? We already are very well acquainted.'

'I am not Arghol.'

'No?'

The good-natured smug certitude offended him.

This man would never see anyone but Arghol he knew.— Yet he on his side saw a man, directly beneath his friend, imprisoned, with intolerable need of recognition.

Arghol, that the baffling requirements of society had made,
impudent parasite of his solitude, had foregathered too long
with men, and bore his name too variously, to be superseded.

He was not sure, if they had been separated surgically, in
which self life would have gone out and in which remained.

'This man has been masquerading as me.'

He repudiated Arghol, nevertheless.

If eyes of his friends-up-till-then could not be opened, he
would sweep them, along with Arghol, into rubbish heap.

Arghol was under a dishonouring pact with all of them.
He repudiated it and him.

'So I am Arghol.'

'Of course. But if you don't want—.'

'That is a lie. Your foolish grin proves you are lying. Good
day.'

Walking on, he knew his friend was himself. He had divested
himself of something.

The other steps followed, timidly and deliberately: odious
invitation.

The sound of the footsteps gradually sent him to sleep.

Next, a Café; he, alone, writing at table.

He became slowly aware of his friends seated at other end
of room, watching him, as it had actually happened before his
return to his uncle's house. There he was behaving as a complete stranger with a set of men he had been on good terms
with two days before.

'He's gone mad. Leave him alone,' they advised each other.

As an idiot, too, he had come home; dropped, idle and
sullen, on his relative's shoulders.

VI.

Suddenly, through confused struggles and vague successions
of scenes, a new state of mind asserted itself.

A riddle had been solved.

What could this be?

He was Arghol once more.

Was that a key to something? He was simply Arghol.

'I am Arghol.'

He repeated his name—like sinister word invented to launch

a new Soap, in gigantic advertisement—toilet-necessity, he, to scrub the soul.

He had ventured in his solitude and failed. Arghol he had imagined left in the city.—Suddenly he had discovered Arghol who had followed him, in Hanp. Always à deux!

———

Flung back to extremity of hut, Hanp lay for some time recovering. Then he thought. Chattel for rest of mankind, Arghol had brutalized him.

Both eyes were swollen pulp.

Shut in: thought for him hardly possible so cut off from visible world.

Sullen indignation at Arghol ACTING, he who had not the right to act. Violence in him was indecent: again question of taste.

How loathsome heavy body, so long quiet, flinging itself about: face strained with intimate expression of act of love.

Firm grip still on him; outrage.

'Pudeur,' in races accustomed to restraint, is the most violent emotion, in all its developments. Devil ridicule, heroism of vice, ideal, god of taste. Why has it not been taken for root of great Northern tragedy?

Arghol's unwieldy sensitiveness, physical and mental, made him a monster in his own eyes, among other things. Such illusion, imparted with bullet-like directness to a companion, falling on suitable soil, produced similar conviction.

This humility of perverse asceticism opposed to vigorous animal glorification of self.

He gave men one image with one hand, and at same time a second, its antidote, with the other.

He watched results a little puzzled.

The conflict never ended.

Shyness and brutality, chief ingredients of their drama, fought side by side.

Hanp had been 'ordered off,' knocked about. Now he was going. Why? Because he had been sent off like a belonging.

Arghol had dragged him down: had preached a certain life, and now insolently set an example of the opposite.

Played with, debauched by a mind that could not leave passion in another alone.

Where should he go? Home. Good natured drunken mother, recriminating and savage at night.

Hanp had almost felt she had no right to be violent and resentful, being weak when sober. He caught a resemblance to present experiences in tipsy life stretching to babyhood.

He saw in her face a look of Arghol.

How disgusting she was, his own flesh. Ah! That was the sensation! Arghol, similarly disgusted through this family feeling, his own flesh: though he was not any relation.

Berlin and nearer city was full of Arghol. He was comfortable where he was.

Arghol had lived for him, worked: impaired his will. Even wheel-making had grown difficult, whereas Arghol acquitted himself of duties of trade quite easily.

WHOSE energy did he use?

Just now the blows had leapt in his muscles towards Arghol, but were sickened and did not seem hard. Would he never be able again to hit? Feel himself hard and distinct on somebody else?

That mass, muck, in the corner, that he hated: was it hoarded energy, stolen or grabbed, which he could only partially use, stagnating?

Arghol was brittle, repulsive and formidable through this sentiment.

Had this passivity been holy, with charm of a Saint's?

Arghol was glutted with others, in coma of energy.

He had just been feeding on him—Hanp!

He REFUSED to act, almost avowedly to infuriate: prurient contempt.

His physical strength was obnoxious: muscles affecting as flabby fat would in another.

Energetic through self-indulgence.

Thick sickly puddle of humanity, lying there by door.

Death, taciturn refrain of his being.

Preparation for Death.

Tip him over into cauldron in which he persistently gazed: see what happened!

This sleepy desire leapt on to young man's mind, after a hundred other thoughts—clown in the circus, springing on horse's back, when the elegant riders have hopped, with obsequious dignity down gangway.

VII.

Bluebottle, at first unnoticed, hurtling about, a snore rose quietly on the air.

Drawn out, clumsy, self-centred! It pressed inflexibly on Hanp's nerve of hatred, sending hysteria gyrating in top of diaphragm, flooding neck.

It beckoned, filthy, ogling finger.

The first organ note abated. A second at once was set up: stronger, startling, full of loathsome unconsciousness.

It purred a little now, quick and labial. Then virile and strident again.

It rose and fell up centre of listener's body, and along swollen nerves, peachy, clotted tide, gurgling back in slimy shallows. Snoring of a malodorous, bloody, sink, emptying its water.

More acutely, it plunged into his soul with bestial regularity, intolerable besmirching.

Aching with disgust and fury, he lay dully, head against ground. At each fresh offence the veins puffed faintly in his temples.

All this sonority of the voice that subdued him sometimes: suddenly turned bestial in answer to his vision.

'How can I stand it! How can I stand it!'

His whole being was laid bare: battened on by this noise. His strength was drawn raspingly out of him. In a minute he would be a flabby yelling wreck.

Like a sleek shadow passing down his face, the rigour of his discomfort changed, sly volte-face of Nature.

Glee settled thickly on him.

The snore crowed with increased loudness, glad, seemingly, with him; laughing that he should have at last learnt to appreciate it. A rare proper world if you understand it!

He got up, held by this foul sound of sleep, in dream of action. Rapt beyond all reflection, he would, martyr, relieve the world of this sound.

Cut out this noise like a cancer.

He swayed and groaned a little, peeping through patches of tumified flesh, boozer collecting his senses; fumbled in pocket.

His knife was not there.

He stood still wiping blood off his face.

Then he stepped across shed to where fight had occurred.

The snore grew again: its sonorous recoveries had amazing and startling strength. Every time it rose he gasped, pressing back a clap of laughter.

With his eyes, it was like looking through goggles.

He peered round carefully, and found knife and two coppers where they had slipped out of his pocket a foot away from Arghol.

He opened the knife, and an ocean of movements poured into his body. He stretched and strained like a toy wound up.

He took deep breaths: his eyes almost closed. He opened one roughly with two fingers, the knife held stiffly at arm's length.

He could hardly help plunging it in himself, the nearest flesh to him.

He now saw Arghol clearly: knelt down beside him.

A long stout snore drove his hand back. But the next instant the hand rushed in, and the knife sliced heavily the impious meat. The blood burst out after the knife.

Arghol rose as though on a spring, his eyes glaring down on Hanp, and with an action of the head, as though he were about to sneeze. Hanp shrank back, on his haunches. He over-balanced, and fell on his back.

He scrambled up, and Arghol lay now in the position in which he had been sleeping.

There was something incredible in the dead figure, the blood sinking down, a moist shaft, into the ground. Hanp felt friendly towards it.

There was only flesh there, and all our flesh is the same. Something distant, terrible and eccentric, bathing in that milky snore, had been struck and banished from matter.

Hanp wiped his hands on a rag, and rubbed at his clothes for a few minutes, then went out of the hut.

The night was suddenly absurdly peaceful, trying richly to please him with gracious movements of trees, and gay processions of arctic clouds.

Relief of grateful universe.

A rapid despair settled down on Hanp, a galloping blackness of mood. He moved quickly to outstrip it, perhaps.

Near the gate of the yard he found an idle figure. It was his master. He ground his teeth almost in this man's face, with an aggressive and furious movement towards him. The face looked shy and pleased, but civil, like a mysterious domestic.

Hanp walked slowly along the canal to a low stone bridge.

His face was wet with tears, his heart beating weakly, a boat slowed down.

A sickly flood of moonlight beat miserably on him, cutting empty shadow he could hardly drag along.

He sprang from the bridge clumsily, too unhappy for instinctive science, and sank like lead, his heart a sagging weight of stagnant hatred.

THE IDEAL GIANT

By WYNDHAM LEWIS

THE IDEAL GIANT

The Action occurs in the Restaurant Gambetta, in German London, in October, 1914. Belgian 'refugees' have found it out in numbers; the poor ones do not get so far. These people are very composed.

The Restaurant is French in its staff and traditions. An Austrian, at present, keeps it.

A cream-lace curtain, hanging from brass hooks, runs all along its face, shoulder high.

A very large brass vase in the middle, and a Russian wood-painting of a Virgin and Child on narrow wall between the two windows, gives the German cultured touch.

The peculiar situation of this Restaurant makes it indispensable to a few people.

The Proprietor is interesting.

The Proprietor follows his stomach about the Restaurant constantly while the Action is proceeding, playing with it like a large ball. He comes right up to John Porter Kemp often and then at the last moment whisks it away, and wheels in another direction, head thrown back, with heroic contraction of brows like a Russian dancer.

FIRST SCENE.
Characters:
MR JOHN FINGAL.
MR JOHN PORTER KEMP.

The Restaurant is behind the two central figures in each scene. The dialogues occur in a little brightly-lighted box at the front of the stage. It is a recess at the back of the Restaurant, which is seen behind it in a perfectly square frame made by the limits of the recess. The box-like recess is painted shiny white with large brass hooks to the left for the coats.

It is sanitary, doll-like and conventional.

Fingal's sienna brown suit, and Kemp's rather vivid blue, under the bright electric light, and Miss Godd's green jersey in 3rd scene, add to the appearance of freshness and artificial bloom.

SCENE I.

MR JOHN FINGAL *is found seated at table, on left-hand side, his right-hand profile to you. He is reading a green evening paper.*

Mr John Fingal is a robust, un-English-looking Adonis, like rank and file stocky Paris cubist; jowl, phlegm, professional classes. He is thirty-six, a solid adventurer, studying art. He does a little dealing. He is flippant, and methodically aggressive in a snobbish way. He sees himself as 'fine old gentleman,' très fin; also as a beautiful young man, the memory of personal triumphs at Cambridge maintained.

He likes speaking French. He does so with careful clumsiness and only so much attempt at a good accent as is compatible with dignity and comfort.

The tables beyond in the body of the Restaurant are occupied by various people, chiefly Belgians.

JOHN PORTER KEMP *comes in from street at far end of stage. He is tall, dog-lean, in first bloom of middle age.*

He is a writer; journalism takes up most of his time.

(Red-haired people seem mongrels—common to every country, like women. Kemp's is a shabby strong mixture, giving him rather a colonial entrée into the civilized world. It carries him back, down the ages, in any case, in an energetic ancestral trail, without the interruptions you must always count on with colourless crops.)

FINGAL *looks up toward the back of stage, and with immediate concentration makes a sign to Kemp, and kicks the chair back on the other side of the table.*

FINGAL. Hallo. Come here, have lunch here—

KEMP. Good morning. What's the news?

FINGAL. In here, do you mean?

> *(Fingal shakes the paper.)*

KEMP. Yes.

> *(Kemp sits down. He does not prune himself, rub his cheeks or hands, or stretch his eyelids. He looks at Menu.)*

FINGAL. Oh. I don't know. Much the same.

KEMP. You've seen the Goeben's been doing something again?

> *(Fingal glances across paper.)*

FINGAL. Yes.

> *(Kemp orders his dinner. A duck and potatoes and salsifis arrive for Fingal. Kemp stares at the Belgians at the*

back of the Restaurant, his large raw eye full of pleasure,
like a golden patine.)
FINGAL. Did you get that book alright?
KEMP. Yes. They hadn't got it at the Times Book Club. I
went to the Figaro. They got it for me. What a nice family that
is over there! How shiny their faces are! They really are nice
greasy lumps.
        (*Fingal looks round at Belgian family, sees what he*
        expected after a minute, and laughs. Kemp turns back to
        the table.)
KEMP. I wish we were more like that. At least I wish we had
that air of being in a tavern they have; or just come out of a
heavy bedroom, like immense dolls out of the box of an erotic
game. They don't mind dying as much as we do, because their
blood is the same oil as the Earth's. With them continuity is
not so broken by demise.
FINGAL. You are romancing.
KEMP. Of course I'm not. Look at Cézanne's race and then
look at us. See how much harder they work at getting their
children! Their pictures, too. But it doesn't show so much in
our children.
FINGAL. Do they? I should have thought—
KEMP. They are much more like the things they eat. They
all have a good deal of pig, horse and dog in them. They yap
and snort and their noses sniff and twitch.
FINGAL. Do you want to be like a pig?
KEMP. It might improve me. I should be willing to try it.
        (*They laugh with indulgence and digestive grace.*)
FINGAL. Are you doing much work? I saw you were writing
in the *London Monthly* the other day. I intended to get it.
KEMP. Yes. There's no reviewing now, during the war. I shall
have to turn strategist, I suppose. I shall not make a good one. I
can never make head or tail of what they're doing over there.
FINGAL. Aren't they going to begin to print other news
again soon?
KEMP. Heaven knows.
        (*A duck and boiled potatoes and salsifis arrive for*
        Kemp: a bottle of Teinach. Fingal's are taken away; The
        garçon is built compactly for body service. His eyes are
        round and blue, and bring to mind Swiss Lakes and mean
        popular sentimentalities. He is your respectful friend and

abject servant. He bends down and advises with a candour and carefulness that make you turn your head away. He stares into the distance when he is not busy. This is his menial cachet.)

KEMP. I wonder if any of these Belgians have been ruined? I expect it is chiefly the working people who have been done for.

FINGAL. I tried to get a Refugee the other day to come and work for me. My little servant girl is going away. I couldn't find one for love or money.

KEMP. I suppose the poor ones get looked after, and drafted off as soon as they arrive.

(*A Pêche Melba is brought for Fingal.*)

KEMP. What is that? Pêche Melba? I must have that. Albert! A Pêche Melba.

FINGAL. Our friend Radac here is pretty busy.

KEMP. If things become very bad I shall get Radac to take me on as garçon. I should enjoy inducting food into those mouths.

(*A Pêche Melba is brought to Kemp.*)

FINGAL. Miss Godd was here yesterday.

KEMP. Was she? But damn Miss Godd.

FINGAL. Damn Miss Godd? She was here about two. Just after you'd gone.

KEMP. I know. I saw her last night.

(*Fingal smiles, but keeps temperately within that demonstration. Miss Godd is a mystery. Fingal has not been asked to meet her. He does not know in what relation Miss Godd and Kemp stand to each other. He sees them at the Restaurant gesticulating in the distance. Kemp does not encourage communication on the subject of his friend. Kemp exaggerates his appetite. Nature with him substituted food for drink as a stimulant. A little food is enough. He has not a strong head. Rendered abnormally communicative and aggressive by the duck and other food, his eye more and more often approaches Fingal, with a progressive ritual like that of a large fly. At last it settles full in the middle of his face. In a few minutes he is grinning at him, talking, twitching his great animal's nose as though it had been surrounded by Grauben gnats.*)

KEMP. Do you sleep well?

FINGAL. Not really well. I vary. I sometimes sleep for eight hours right off, sometimes only four. My average is a bit below the necessary, I should say.

(This punctilious answer was in order to save time, and was the result of experience of Kemp. Kemp and Fingal's talks resembled those arranged between the Proprietor of the Circus and the Clown. Fingal would display the meticulous credulity of the toff in evening dress. Kemp does not want to know, however, about Fingal's powers of sleep. It is one of his feints. This is his way of 'working.')

KEMP. Are you sensitive about your shell?

FINGAL. No. No.

KEMP. The husk you shed at night?

FINGAL. Ah. No.

(Kemp pulls his chair forward a little and leans across the table. He constantly shoots his eye up, while speaking, at an imaginary third person in the middle distance. Sometimes he fixes this myth with his blank red-rimmed disk of an eye, and stops his discourse. Or he will lower his voice as though to prevent this third person from overhearing his most harmless remarks.)

KEMP. Life for some people is full of the nuisance of symmetries and forms. When you put your pen down, do you begin worrying about its position in relation to the inkpot?

FINGAL. I can't say I do.

KEMP. *Some people*—have a certain personal arrangement with their clothes at night. This is very common. I, for myself, have to tie my bootlaces symmetrically. Have you never stepped in every second or third stone of a pavement, and been afflicted if you were compelled to miss one? I know a man who walked all the way back from Oxford Circus to Waring and Gillows to plant his foot on a stone he had been compelled to miss!

FINGAL. That is bad neurasthenia, isn't it?

KEMP. Of course. And therefore should be fought and broken up from time to time.

FINGAL. I agree with you.

(Kemp sits back in his chair as though his bolt were shot, and the argument closed. This is more feinting and personal play of his high-spirits. He then comes forward again in his chair.)

KEMP. Truth, at all events, is a thing like that. Our truthfulness. Some people—have an uneasiness and sense of something wrong, out of place, crying to be put right, if they have been compelled or have elected to tell an untruth. There is something in such and such a person's mind, placed there by them, that should not be there. Or it should not be there in that form. It is 'the thing which is not' of the Horses.

(*Kemp draws a cigar out of his pocket, cuts the end off, and lights it.*)

KEMP. This meticulous sense will induce a man to describe very carefully something he has seen, if he describes it at all, and to suffer if, from laziness or other motive, he has slurred or misrepresented. This is the common base of wisdom and beauty. It is the famous generic madness at the bottom of genius.

It is the madness known as 'Exactitude' in America.

(*Kemp fixes Fingal with his eye, Ancient Mariner fashion, and shows him by a pause, that the preamble is over. He takes several deep breaths, inhaling his very bad cigar. Fingal disturbs the manoeuvring of his eye.*)

FINGAL. What would the clever Horses find to call your stories? Those 'things that are not' fill your brains.

KEMP. The transference is so complete in creative life of any sort. *Reality* is the 'thing which is not,' for the creative artists. An artist would have precisely that feeling of 'malaise' and disgust if he had put in another man's head the *real truth*— the actual biological appearance of Nature, that my ideally truthful man would feel if he had lied.

FINGAL. The arranging of the clothes; or the symmetry of the bootlace; is a sign of a feeling for order. Whereas the squeamishness about 'the truth' in another man's head is a slavish timidity.

KEMP. I don't think so. I don't see the contradiction. In the sphere of practical life it is essential to have facts. People can only base their actions on facts. If you put in a person's head something purporting to be a fact, which is not a fact, it is liable to cause the utmost confusion and disorder.

But the point of my argument is the *physical* uneasiness about this thing said, whether fact or not, the 'hallucination of the Object.'

The 'truth' is only another way of saying 'the substantial.' In life the 'substantial' is the 'fact.'

FINGAL. I'm afraid I don't see what you're driving at.

(*Gruff and cold contemplation from the lofty general entrenched beside Kemp's nose, conducting the affairs of the world, ensues. The eye sweeps over Fingal slowly like a searchlight.*)

KEMP. Do you tell many lies?

(*Kemp fixes his eye stonily.*)

FINGAL (*grinning*). Sometimes. But I'm a particular man. I am an esprit d'ordre.

KEMP. I am the same. I am the same—I never lie—

(*Kemp beams, in sudden immense thawing. A pause, in which Kemp inundates Fingal with smiles of nauseating richness. Renewed pretence that this is the bourne of his argument: namely, that he never tells lies.*)

FINGAL. Garçon. L'addition s'il vous plaît.

(*Fingal accepts this feint, and prepares to break up the séance. The waiter comes, and stooping down to the table, makes up the bill.*)

WAITER. Attendez. Il y avait deux légumes.

FINGAL. Oui. Un salsifis.

WAITER. Oh yes. Salsifis. Thank you Mr Fingal.

(*Fingal pays the bill, but does not at once get up. Kemp leans forward and puts his hand on Fingal's arm.*)

KEMP. Today I have been lying steadily ever since I got up. The last two or three times we've met, I have told you several lies; which you did not notice.

I feel as though I should never tell the truth again.

(*Kemp sits back and stares at Fingal.*)

FINGAL. I noticed all your lies, and was distressed.

KEMP. That is not true.

FINGAL. Oh yes. Perfectly. You told me you paid twopence each for those cigars.

KEMP. Well, so I did.

FINGAL. Am I to take that as a lie; or, to put it another way, regard it as a proof, under the circumstances, that you did not pay that for them?

KEMP. I paid twopence for this excellent cigar.

(*Kemp holds it up, and blows out his gingercream cheeks at its gilded label.*)

FINGAL. Then why did you tell—?

(*Kemp springs up and calls the waiter.*)

KEMP. Bring me a 'Flor de Cijas'.

(*He throws his cigar away, sits down and holds up his finger, then hooks it over his nose. He has seen some fat mid-European man with a cigar do this, and the fact of his smoking a cigar, habit to which he has lately taken, suggests this action.*)

KEMP. I am found out. This will not make me downhearted. As a matter of fact I do not mind being found out. That is not material. I am not setting out to deceive, but only to cure myself of a superstition and rigid manner of feeling.

(*While handling Radac's much more satisfactory cigar, Kemp explains his latest regimen.*)

KEMP. For instance, this arm of mine attracted attention this morning.

(*His arm is bandaged, and cased in a black leather trough which he takes off to eat. Kemp is getting over blood-poisoning in the wrist and forearm.*)

KEMP. I posed as a Mons hero, with this, yesterday evening, in a pub. It was a triumph for me. Education and natural integrity revolt against that stupid action. We will admit it is not in my line. But I am too shy. Such things are excellent discipline. They harden, humble and invigorate. They are a medicine made up of the acrid harshness of the flash scum of a city.

The Ego's worst enemy is Truth. This gives Truth the slap in the face good for us.

(*The Proprietor approaches; stands in the middle of the square opening, his stomach pointing rudely at them, head and eye frowning down on Kemp. They look at him in silence. He suddenly whisks his stomach away, wheels, and moves shoulderingly back into the restaurant.*)

KEMP (*continuing*). Self. Self. One must rescue that sanity. Truth, duty—are insanity.

FINGAL. You are talking for the times. There are times when Self, Self—

KEMP. Yes, perhaps. But if we have not War, we have Art—

FINGAL. Now we have both—

KEMP. But Art is much the purer and stronger, and against its truths and impositions we much revolt or at least react. The 'pure artist' is a Non-sense.

The gentleman, likewise, must be shown his place.

The Prussian exploits the psychology of the commis-voyageur to harden himself into a practical aggressor—

FINGAL. Do not let us be like the Prussian, for—

KEMP. Heaven forbid; ah yes, forbid. We could not be if we tried. We therefore could introduce a little of his methods without the danger he runs of foolishness and vulgarity.

FINGAL. What exactly do you want us to do?

KEMP. I was talking about the individual. The Nation nowadays always has as much vulgarity as it can stand.

FINGAL. Quite. Then you mean—

KEMP. We, as individuals, are at a disadvantage in a struggle with the community. It contains, invariably, inevitably, criminal energy, stoicism and vulgarity of a high order.

FINGAL. But why do you make this opposition between the individual and the community?

KEMP. *I* did not make it.

FINGAL. But does it exist to the extent you—?

KEMP. It exists. It exists like this. A hundred men is a giant.

(*Kemp makes his points with a finger flattened out on the table. The Proprietor brings his stomach forward. Kemp waves it hurriedly away with his flat, stiff finger.*)

KEMP. A hundred men is a giant. A giant is always rather lymphatic and inclined to be weak intellectually, we are told. He is also subject to violent rages. Just as legendary men were always at war with the giants, so are individuals with society.

That exceptional men can be spoilt by the world is a commonplace. But consider another thing. See how two or three distinguished people lose personal value in a mob—at a dinner, at a meeting. Their personalities deteriorate in a moment—for an hour or two. They hardly ever become the head and brain of the Giant.

FINGAL. That doesn't apply to all men? It is due to some weakness in the personality. Some shine most.

KEMP. Ah, yes. But examine those shiners by themselves, and look steadily at their words and acts. Theirs is a practical and relative success. The *solitary* test is the only searching one. The fine personality loses, in every case, by association. *The problem in life is to maintain the Ideal Giant.*

The artist is the Ideal Giant or Many. The Crowd at its moments of heroism also is. But Art is never at its best without the assaults of Egotism and of Life.

For the health of the Giant as much as for that of the individual this conflict and its alertes are necessary.

Revolution is the normal proper state of things.

FINGAL. Paraguay or Venezuela offering the picture of the Ideal State.

KEMP. They are not States. They are just Revolutions. They should be called the 'Revolution of Venezuela,' etcetera, etcetera.

(*Fingal leans back against the wall and stretches.*)

FINGAL. Well, as though we hadn't war enough already! Here you are trying to stir up a new war—a World-War, too, I suppose.

KEMP. No, I'm afraid one war might make us forget our other wars.

FINGAL. I wish it would!

(*Fingal stares back into the Restaurant. Two tables away a stout Belgian woman is eating, with her leg heavily bandaged resting on a chair. Kemp turns towards Restaurant, pivoting on his chair, one elbow on table.*)

KEMP. Did the Germans do that?

FINGAL. No. She comes from Louvain, but she did that herself.

KEMP. Has not she the grace to attribute it to the Germans? She comes from Louvain, bandaged, at a moment like this! It is a case for the police. She must be in German pay.

FINGAL. Quite likely. And as we are the only people she impresses—

(*The Proprietor approaches from door at left.*)

THE PROPRIETOR. Miss Godd wishes to speak to you on the telephone.

(*Kemp gets up.*)

KEMP. I must go and telephone.

(*Fingal gets up.*)

FINGAL. I must go.

KEMP. I shall see you soon again, perhaps?

FINGAL. Yes. I'm going North for a few days. I shall be back the beginning of next week.

(*They both walk back into Restaurant, Kemp going out through door at left, half way down the wall, Fingal through street door at farther end of Restaurant.*)

SCENE II.
Characters:
MR JOHN PORTER KEMP.

Scene: A dark recess, about 6 feet long, with a telephone desk on wall, on which John Kemp is leaning and speaking at telephone. At the back is a staircase, on which several people go up and down during action. His nose occasionally obscures the telephone mouthpiece as he bends his head and listens. When he answers his nose seems fighting and fuming, or drawing itself up solemnly, admonishing the mouth into which he is speaking. His face is red, the veins protruding on the side of his forehead, partly from the effect of holding the earpiece up to his ear.

KEMP. No, I did not say that. What I meant was that honesty was a rhythm; it must be broken up. I found myself becoming the first cousin to George Washington. I really *couldn't* tell a lie! I became the slave of any bloody fact. Similarly, but oppositely, in my writing. *I did not introduce a single real character taken from life, for over a year!* I was becoming in both cases a *maniac*. In the case of art: a man I met every day in the Restaurant might coincide, except for some irrelevant details, with my last dream or will-picture! But I steered all round him askance, and never touched him, as though he had been a ghost! He was something, I felt, that was too true to be true. Do you see? Not to consider life partially a dream, or fancy partially a substance, is utter madness! My fancies are so matter-of-fact, shameless and conceited, that they march about the streets like Golyadkin's double. I have refused to accept them as *real*, up till now, simply because they happened to be *there*! It is absurd! What? Absurd!

(Kemp inclines his head and listens crossly. The voice speaking in his ear evidently annoys him.)

KEMP. Yes. I mentioned Golyadkin: he—but that is wandering from the point.

(His face becomes a confused mass of irony, shame, and irritation.)

KEMP. Your father's spoons are excellent. Yes. That shows the right spirit. But it is not by pawning a spoon. What?

(Kemp seems no longer listening. He says, 'What!' occasionally and then relapses into staring at the ground. He at last begins speaking with impatient emphasis;

putting two more pennies into the machine.)

KEMP. My point is plain. It is entirely a question of whole hogging, and escaping from the dreariness and self-contempt of *play*. We *play* at everything here—at love, art, winning and losing—don't we? We do! The artists: take *them*! They are the rottenest and most contemptible crowd discoverable—rotten as most artists-crowds are, anywhere in the world; one of the worst sort of crowds. Chelsea! It is a name today that does not leave us many memories, alas, of genuinely Guinevere-loving able dreamers. It is the most pestiferous haunt of dilettantism, snobbery and bourgeois selfishness. Consider that 'rag' we went to last week! Oh my God! But all that we are agreed on. Now, at least all *that* we must not be! How shall we avoid becoming that play-acting, bickering, pretending trash? Easily, for you require years of selfish nursing to become that. You say: When there is fire and intelligence and will all round you, you will become modelled to a reality that spits on that! Your quiet will not be contaminated: your dreaming will ignore the mess in which it sits and contrives. Not quite! We owe ourselves a sacrifice. I would rather be out there with the soldiers than here with the playmen of the—Western World! But when you think of battles you cannot help remembering that it is that art-crowd that are being fought for, instead of the 'Our women and children' for whom you are to 'lend our strong right arm.' Women can always look after themselves, can't they?

'*We are the civilization for which you are fighting!*' I read today in a newspaper that one of the 'Café Royalties', as the delighted paper called them, had said that. And then, having uttered that boast, he departed to a studio-rag; and the next morning he sculpted his daily sculp, or pawed on to his canvas his daily slop, probably German as regards its emotions and intelligence; indubitably vomit. No! action, for me, does not lie that way. And then again if you don't remember the art-crowd, you remember other equally nauseous ones that linger behind and contaminate the War, actually dirtying with their existence the bitterest heroism, degrading death. Yet *action*, if you could find the right action, is the 'sovereign cure for our ills.'

And it is maddening to live with such a profusion of action suddenly poured out, most wasted; at least not curing what requires that cure.

(*Kemp places two more pennies in the box, muttering,* '*what porridge had John Keats?*' *He seems pursuing some parallel between his oratory and the pennies.*)

KEMP. Yes. Well then, I doubt if you *can* act now, in the sense I mean, any more than you can swim without water. But at least avoid degrading *substitutes* for action. If you act, in however slight a way, *act*. If you are not *doing* anything, do not pretend that you are. Do *nothing*. It is the only clean proceeding when conditions are against some particular form of action. Do not shrink from misfortune. It will not hurt you. Then—I can hold this thing no longer to my ear. I must go, as well. Are you at your father's house? Alone? I shouldn't interfere with his property any more! Ha! Ha! We meet tomorrow. Farewell.

(*Kemp places the receiver up, and walks quickly back through the door into the Restaurant.*)

SCENE III.
(Same as Scene I. Time: next day, 1.30.)
Characters:
MR JOHN PORTER KEMP.
MISS ROSE GODD.
Detective: WILLIAM DRUCE.

Rose Godd and Kemp are sitting opposite each other at table. Rose Godd is a very large-boned flatfaced woman of twenty years. When she stands up she is very tall and strong looking, with a small head and thick neck. The Mongol intensity of her face is mitigated by self-consciousness. Her lips are painted a bright red in the midst of her yellow skin. She is always perfectly calm. She feels that her intelligence is not quite good enough for her company: but pride in what she considers her latent power of action brings her into steadfastness. Kemp, as he looks at her, wonders sometimes whether the 'action' he preaches will not be found in his case in Rose Godd flinging herself on him and trying to tear him to pieces. But he is satisfied, on reflection (and turns from the fact with distaste, usually) that it is a softer conflict that she desires. But as between Rose Godd and himself that action could not be disguised into the rôle of discovery.

KEMP. Will you have coffee? Albert! Two coffees please!

WAITER. Two coffees, sir? Yes sir!

KEMP. That is the situation and there is no preamble. But Hakluyt travelled into lands we could never discover. He went on millions of leagues further than we could ever go. We are thrown back on ourselves in that sense. That is *action*. The old way: something divorced from ourselves: the appetite for, and the conditions to attain to, the New. To fit out a high wooden ship, with a poop and a carved figure on the bow, at Plymouth, to sail for El Dorado or even Rio Grande, would be neither venturesome nor intelligent. It would be a reconstruction as foolish as Don Quixote's was wise. Yet we suffer from this shrivelling up of our horizons. We need those horizons, and action and adventure as much as our books need exercise. We have been rendered sedentary by perfected transport. Our minds have become home-keeping. We do not *think* as boldly: our thoughts do not leap out in the same way.

Well, in the case of the Earth there is nothing to be done. If it were suddenly increased to twenty times its present size we should not be impressed, or see Giants now, intellectual or other. That something subtle and multitudinous that is the Poet, is not so easy to describe: for to say that he is 'great' is not the point, although it satisfied our Victorian forefathers to see him as a perfect, very big, and muscular *man*, with philological credentials, a König, a canny-man: a Can-Man. He was a cloud-squatting Jehovah's athletic twin brother. Then when we hear this war referred to as 'the Greatest War of all time,' we laugh irritably. It is not by a counting of heads, or poor corpses, that the blank in our imagination can be filled! They were evil fellows who stole our visions. He would be a great saviour who could get them back again! Meantime it is a female's game to go on pretending this, and playing at that! We must contrive; find a new Exit. Any wildly subversive action should be welcomed. *We must escape from the machine in ourselves! Smash it up: renew ourselves.*

(*The Proprietor brings his stomach slowly up. It appears like an emblem of the Earth to Kemp, who points to it with a fork as a schoolmaster might, at a class-room globe. But it has come too late. Miss Godd and Kemp stare stupidly at it together. They at last begin laughing, and Radac carries it swiftly away, frowning over his shoulder.*)

KEMP. But I think you misunderstood me with your spoons!

(*He smiles slowly and archly at her, wagging his head. She looks at him with such fixity that his smile is gradually driven off his face. He remains staring at her in a sobered, cross, astonishment.*)

KEMP. I am sorry. Have I hurt you? Did you put much store in the spoons?

(*She shakes her head. Two or three tears roll down her cheeks.*)

KEMP. But your spoons are no more ineffective than my lies. What did you get for them?

MISS GODD. Not much.

KEMP. No. There's not much demand for spoons, I suppose.

MISS GODD. Not much.

(*Kemp looks down at his plate. Their entente today does not seem the same as on other occasions. Her face appears at once reproachful, insolently claiming something, antagonistically reserved. She appears looking at him out of armour in which she has implicit confidence. Kemp is embarrassed, and when he begins speaking again takes up the subject truculently. He attributes her attitude, for want of a better explanation, to his reasoning. He feels he has not held his audience.*)

KEMP. I feel that my lies and your spoons were about as playful as some of the absurdities with which we reproach our art-friends. Compared to death on a barricade, or the robber Garnier's Swedish exercises while he was in hiding in the suburbs of Paris, they are slight exploits. The blood that spurts from a tapped proboscis is not enough. A spoon will not thrust you into jail for so long that you forget what the Earth looks like. For the hair to turn white, the heart to turn grey, in an hour, you require the real thing, ma mie.

MISS GODD. Yes.

(*Kemp looks at her sideways. Her face is green and her eyes shining. He reverts once more to the hypothesis of a wrestling-match with Rose Godd. He looks at her large muscular hands. She follows the direction of his eyes. With a sudden look of panic she places them under the table, and between her knees, and she seems almost hissing at him.*)

MISS GODD. What are you looking at, Kemp? What are you looking at?

KEMP. At your hands.

(*She works them up and down spasmodically as if they were cold.*)

KEMP. But 'it is the principle.' A great violence, unless you were sure you had your finger on the spot, would be no better. So long as you are *pretending* to do anything desperate or the reverse. The objective I indicate is different. Whether it is extreme or puerile is as it happens.

MISS GODD. As it happens?

KEMP. You seem rather odd, Miss *Godd*!

MISS GODD. Give me a cigarette.

KEMP. You ask for it like a criminal on the scaffold!

(*He gives Miss Godd a cigarette. A man has entered the door of the Restaurant. He is talking to Radac, the Proprietor. Kemp watches him idly for a moment. He then notices that the Proprietor and the newcomer are both looking at the table where Rose Godd and himself are seated. He glances over to Rose Godd, and finds her eyes are fixed on him, with a senseless fiery questioning.*)

KEMP. What is the matter?

MISS GODD. Nothing. I wondered something—But your standards are so high!

KEMP. I can't help my standards being a bit cocked up.

MISS GODD. I mean in this respect: in connection with what we talk about so much.

KEMP. What?—

MISS GODD. You must torment me with your denseness. Your standards for *action* are so difficult. You won't accept an action. You look at an action as critically as you do at a thought. Most actions won't stand that. They are delicate little things, or rough undeveloped things, or mad things. If you *look* at them too hard—as that man is looking at me—(*Miss Godd indicates the man who is talking to Radac*) they might shrivel up, they do get small. I *pity* all actions. They are so unimportant compared to thought. For all their blood, men sniff at them and dissect them.

KEMP. There need not be blood.

MISS GODD. You don't have to dig far for blood.

(*Radac and the man who has been talking to him have come up, and are standing a few yards from the table now, listening to the conversation of Kemp and Miss Godd.*)

KEMP. No, it is true. But the avoir-du-poids amount of violence is no criterion of action. It would have taken no more force and would be no more bloody an action, to kill Napoleon than any contemporary bourgeois in France. But it would have been a more important action. And *any* action, however bloodless, that hamstrung that destructive personality, would have been a more important action than to cut a grocer's throat.

MISS GODD. Or a Banker's.

KEMP. Why a Banker?

MISS GODD. Because—he *was* a banker.

KEMP. Who? Napoleon?

MISS GODD. This gentleman will tell you.

(*Miss Godd looks up sideways at the man with Radac.*)

KEMP. What the devil are you standing there for?

DETECTIVE WILLIAM DRUCE. Steady—steady. None of your devils to me, please. *You* may be the Devil, for all I know. I am a Police Officer. You are Miss Rose Godd, I believe?

MISS GODD (*looking at him blackly*). Yes, that's my name.

DETECTIVE WILLIAM DRUCE. I have come to arrest you, Rose Godd, for the murder of Nicolas Godd.

KEMP. Murder! Murder of whom?

MISS GODD (*laughs*). Napoleon!

DETECTIVE WILLIAM DRUCE. Come with me, please.

(*The Detective watches Rose Godd with wary attention. Rose Godd gets up, her face a dark white, her lips hard factitious crimson.*)

MISS GODD. Good-bye!

KEMP. Haven't you—? Is Nicolas Godd your father?

MISS GODD. Good-bye!

KEMP. But you haven't that—that!

MISS GODD. I have acted.

(*The Detective springs at Rose Godd, catching her by the wrists, and a small bottle falls on the table. They roll on the floor together, and the back of the restaurant becomes full of a crowd of people—diners, Radac, and some folk from the street.*

Kemp sits with his white profile, and large eye distorted with shame and perplexity. He springs up, partly disappearing behind the table, where he is noticed to have seized the Detective by the collar.)

CURTAIN

ENEMY OF THE STARS

BY
WYNDHAM LEWIS

DESMOND HARMSWORTH
LONDON
1932

THE PLAY

ONE IS IN IMMENSE COLLAPSE OF CHRONIC PHILO-
SOPHY. YET HE BULGES ALL OVER, COMPLEX FRUIT,
WITH SIMPLE PITH OF LIFE. VENUSTIC AND VERIDIC—
TYPE OF FEMININE BEAUTY CALLED 'MANNISH.' THE
HERO'S PONDEROUS MASK IS OF BEST NORTHERN
WORKMANSHIP.

IT IS HIS AGON. FIRST HE IS ALONE. A HUMAN BULL,
BOOTED AND BLINKERED, RUSHES INTO THE CIRCUS.
THIS IS THROG, OF NO MORE CONSEQUENCE THAN
LOUNGING STAR OVERHEAD. HE IS NOT EVEN A
'STAR.' HE RUSHES OFF, HE CHARGES BACK, INTO THE
DARKNESS BENEATH THE SURFACE OF THE SCENE.

CHARACTERS AND PROPERTIES BOTH EMERGE FROM
A PRECIPITOUS RAMP DESCENDING INTO THE EARTH.
THIS TRAP IS UPON THE CIRCUMFERENCE OF THE PIT
INTO WHICH THE SPECTATORS GAZE—NOTHING BUT
'GALLERY' IN THIS TELESCOPIC STAGECRAFT. THE
PROTAGONIST REMAINS A LONG WHILE NEGLECTED,
AFTER THE INFERNAL ASSAULT, AS THOUGH HIS
FELLOW ACTORS HAD FORGOTTEN HIM, CAROUSING
IN THEIR PROFESSIONAL CAVERN.

*Second Character. Jew-beaked and jag-taloned—a gorcrow,
as sleek and sable—the juvenile apache. Black bourgeois aspirations undermine that blatant virtuosity of self. Criminal
instinct of intemperate bilious heart, the violent underdog, is
put at service of Unknown Humanity, our King. The latter's
boundless royal aversion for the great Protagonist (for the
premier character, whose agon it is—statue-mirage of Liberty
in the great desert) finds expression in the words and attitudes
of this humble locum-tenens.*

*Mask of discontent, anxious to explode (he is restrained by
qualms of vanity). Eyes grown venturesome in native temperatures of Pole—indulgent and familiar, blessing with white nights.*

*Throughout, the type of the characters, very pronounced in
this all-star cast as well, has been selected from those broad
compact faces where Europe grows arctic, intense—human and
universal.*

*['Yet you and me!' I hear you—What of you and me? 'Why
not from the english metropolis?' But in this mad marriage of*

false minds, is not this a sort of honeymoon? We go abroad.
Such a strange thing as our coming together requires a strange
place too for the initial stages of our intimate ceremonious
acquaintance. It is our 'agon' too. Remember that it is our
destiny!]

THERE ARE TWO SCENES
THE STAGE ARRANGEMENTS

RED OF TARNISHED COPPER PREDOMINANT COLOUR.
UP-ENDED EGG-BOXES, CASKS, RUBBLE, CHEVAUX DE
FRISE, COLLECTIONS OF CLAY-LOAM AND BRICK-DUST,
HAVE BEEN COVERED, THROUGHOUT ARENA, WITH
DISUSED SAIL-CANVAS, STAINED AND HENNAED.
  HUT OF SECOND SCENE.— THIS IS SUGGESTED BY
CHARACTERS TAKING UP THEIR POSITION AT THE
OPENING OF THE SHAFT LEADING DOWN INTO MIMES'
QUARTERS. THE COWLS OF TWO UPCASTS, FOR VENTI-
LATION OF LATTER, PROTRUDE TO LEFT OF HATCH-
WAY.
  A GUST, SUCH AS IS MET WITH IN THE CORRIDORS
OF THE UNDERGROUND, CAUSES THEIR CLOTHES TO
SHIVER OR TO FLAP. THIS ARTIFICIAL SUBTERRAN-
EOUS WIND BLARES UP THEIR VOICES—THE MASKS ARE
FITTED WITH TRUMPETS OF ANTIQUE THEATRE—
WITH EFFECT OF TWO CHILDREN BLOWING AT EACH
OTHER WITH TOY INSTRUMENTS OF METAL.
  THE AUDIENCE LOOKS DOWN INTO THE SCENE—AS
THOUGH IT WERE A HUT ROLLED HALF UPON ITS
BACK, DOOR UPWARDS, THE CHARACTERS GIDDILY
MOUNTING IN ITS OPENING.

ARGHOL

INVESTMENT OF RED UNIVERSE.
  EACH FORCE IN TURN ATTEMPTS TO SHAKE HIM. HE
IS ROCKED AND TOSSED—INFLUENCE AFTER INFLU-
ENCE IN SLOW SUCCESSION IS BROUGHT UP TO ASSAIL
HIM, EACH AFTER ITS MANNER.
  CENTRAL AS STONE, THE FIRST PLAYER (THE FIRE-
NAME OF ARGHOL) IS A POISED MAGNET, OF SUBTLE,
VAST, SELFISH THINGS.

WHEN LYING, HE IS THE HUMAN STRATUM OF IN-
FERNAL BIOLOGIES, SILL UPON SILL, HIGHLY COM-
PRESSED. WALKING, HE APPEARS A WARY SHIFTING
OF BODIES IN DISTANT EQUIPOISE. A GOD BUILT BY
AN ARCHITECTURAL STREAM, FECUNDED BY MAD
BLASTS OF SUNLIGHT, SITTING, HE MOST RESEMBLES.
THE LAST POSE BECOMES HIM BEST—THE AFFINITY
WITH THE BUDDHA.

THE ACTION OPENS

*The first stars appear. Arghol comes out of the hut—it is his
cue. The stars are his cast. The player is a matter of thirty
minutes behind time and emerges compulsing into its button-
hole a whalebone disk. A murmur disturbs the cream of Posterity, assembled in silent ranks, generation behind generation. One hears the gnats' song of the Thirtieth Centuries.*

*They strain to see him, the gladiator who has come to do
battle with an ideologic phantom, namely, Humanity. It is the
great popular recreation of the Future Mankind. This is the
outstanding athlete, the prime exponent of this sport in its
palmy days. Posterity slowly sinks into the hypnotic trance of
art; then the arena is transformed into the necessary scene.*

THE RED WALLS OF THE UNIVERSE NOW SHUT THEM
IN, WITH THIS FOREDOOMED PROMETHEUS. THEY
BREATHE IN CLOSE ATMOSPHERE OF TERROR AND
NECESSITY, UNTIL THE EXECUTION IS OVER AND THE
RED WALLS RECEDE—THE DESTINY OF ARGHOL CON-
SUMMATED, THE UNIVERSE SATISFIED!

[*THE BOX OFFICE RECEIPTS HAVE BEEN ENORMOUS.*]

THE YARD

ROUGH EDEN OF ONE SOUL—TO WHOM ANOTHER
MAN, AND NOT EVE, WOULD BE MATED.

THE EARTH HAS BURST, A GRANITE FLOWER, THAT
IT MAY DISCLOSE, IN EARTHQUAKE FASHION, THE
APPOINTED PROSCENIUM.

*A WHEELWRIGHT'S YARD. Once a figure-yard, of the
statuary's trade, there are still the fragments of granite cupids,
and a torso of a horse which has lost its ears and lips. Here are*

the hoops for sport of nurseling giants—the axes of splintered radii, starfish-wise, axletrees, rotted limbers and rusted linch-pins, fasces of spokes. A refuse of chariots—the lumber-place of obsolete equipages, for fashion and for industry.

The yard is full of dry, white volcanic light. It is compact with the emblems of one trade: there are tall stacks of pine—ribbons of iron, wheels stranded. A canal bank traverses one side of the allotted octagon. The night is pouring into it like blood from a butcher's bucket—a red night.

Rouge mask in aluminium mirror—the grimace of sunset through the dark glass of the twilight—it rushes in almost with a faint roar of water. A leaden gob, slipped at zenith, the first drop of violent night. The drop spreads cataclysmically in the harsh waters of evening—caustic Reckitt's stain. The black night comes down on top of the red. The white night follows, with its fierce blue steadfast glare.

Three trees, above the canal—a sentimental black trinity. They are in three sizes, the third is a splendid creature, six feet across the butt. They drive their leaf-flocks, they propel them with jeering cry. They plunge, with their anchored herds. They recover themselves—they hurl themselves forward. They do not fall down. They repeat the trick—with a great gasp of mockery—at their Encore. They shiver erect, all the rout of their foliage swirling upon their bodies. Else they slightly bend their joints, impassible acrobats—step rapidly forward, faintly incline their heads.

Across the mud-in-pod of the canal the shadows of the lofty trees are gawky toy crocodiles (sawed up and down by infant giant?). Gollywog of Arabian symmetry, Arghol drags them in blank nervous hatred. There is a thin moon beneath a puff of blood-red cloud. A merganser comes up out of the patch of opal mist where the recumbent giant is to be attacked and goes to its nest somewhere.

THE SUPER

Arghol is seen to cross the yard, he wanders upon the banks of the canal until he reaches the patch of mist. There he sits down, all but his trunk immersed in the miasma.

'ARGHOL!' *THERE IS A BELLOW OUT OF THE BLACK-NESS BEHIND HIM.*

'I AM HERE,' *HE RESPONDS, IN A STRONG CROAK,
FROM WHERE HE LIES HALF HIDDEN IN THE TERRENE
CLOUDLET.*

*His voice is raucous and disfigured with a catarrh of lies,
contracted in the fetid bankrupt atmosphere of life's swamp—
but clear and splendid among Truth's balsamic hills, shepherding his agile thoughts.*

'ARGHOL!'

*Like the hateful summons of the tiny-tot, hunting its truant,
its dejected, mommer, it breaks out in a rage of incontinence.
Primitive distress sharpens the thick bellowing bluster. Out
rushes the figure—it arrives rushing without running visibly,
as if discharged along the surface of the earth.*

*Arghol heels over upon his left side. It is the female gesture
to facilitate aggression, born of the instinct to reduplicate and
breed. Careened in this fashion, the right-hand ribs thrust up
offered to the blind assault, a jackboot batters them. These are
the least damaged: it is their turn to be struck at, hence his
position.*

*Upper lip shot down, covering half of the black silk chin,
like a tight-fitting cap, his body reaches, with the method
resulting from long-established habit. Upon the receipt of each
crashing kick, in muscular spasm, he makes the pain pass out.
He revolves, contracts and vaults up against the boot—he
crouches and flings his grovelling Enceladus weight against it,
like swimmer with wave.*

*The boot, the heavy shadow above it, passes. With a whistling
noise peculiar to it, the self-centred and elemental shadow
passes softly and sickly into the doorway's brown light.*

*The second attack, in its absence—the pain that is, left by
the first shadow, lashing him—is worse. He loses consciousness,
at this empty repetition—the recollection—the rankling—of the
blackened flesh.*

THE NIGHT

*His eyes wake first, shaken by rough moonbeams. A crude
volume of brute light—blanched, toneless and vivid—blazes in
the planetarium surmounting the narrow arena. He looks up
into this narrow dome. Bleak electric advertisement of God,
sky-sign of the cosmos. An extravagant immensity—with an*

outlay of sheer candle-power—it crushes the onlooker—it oppresses the creature—with wild emptiness of stress.

Arghol meditates, his head out of the mist-patch. The ice-fields of the sky sweep and crash silently overhead. Blowing wild organism out of the mouth of nothing into the hard splendid clouds, some Will casts down its glare, as well, over him. He lies dazzled and still in the silent illuminations.

The canal, that is headed in one direction—his blood, weakly, ploddeth in the opposite. Nature and he pursue opposite paths, in a hostile polarity.—But now the stars shine madly in the archaic blank wilderness of the Universe, machines of prey. Mastodons, placid in electric atmosphere—they are white rivers of power. They stand fixed, in eternal black sunlight. They stand up and sing, louder than the morning, shriller than the firstcomers of the twilight, more profoundly than the foghorn of the sun.

Tigers are beautiful imperfect brutes. The animal beauty of the star-stamped intoxicating heavens is greater than tigers' (for all the head-lights of the killer, muscles of quicksilver)—it is the imperfection much more of the splendour of gods. At the steadfast lightning of this dark storm of worlds the eyes of Arghol wink starwise in sympathy with the effects of a far-offness of long light years.

Throats iron eternities (drinking heavy radiance)—limbs towers of blatant light—the stars poise, stupendously remote. Metal-sided, meteoritic, they are the pantheistic machines fashioned by the astronomer.

The farther, the more violent and vivid, Nature! thinks he, staring back at the flood-lit super-systems. Weakness is crushed out of creation—hard weakness, a flea's size, would be pinched to death in a second could it get so far as that!

Next, truncated by the mist-patch, he has risen to his feet, yawning and swaying—confronting this chill cliff of cadaverous beaming force. Imprisoned in a messed socket of existence, his place in this panorama of power is obscure. He stands, his hands in his stomach-pockets. 'Will it some day,' says he to himself, 'will energy some day reach Earth, like violent civilization descending—smashing or hardening all?' He rocks his head, which blares with the pressures of his charging blood.

In the consciousness however of this giant tenderfoot a chip of distant hardness is tugged at dully like a tooth. This distant pull causes him to ache from crown to toe. But so far the violences of all things have left him intact. He is whole as a stone, the core of erosions.

HANP

Hanp comes up out of the property-hut. He walks slowly, coughing, chopping the air in goatish spasms. He rolls, as he stumbles forward, a ragged cigarette between his uncouth fingers of his hands all thumbs. Thrusting it into the hair-edged hole of his musty mouth, he coughs its smoke out as it collects, and climbs towards the place where Arghol lies, again inert, after a haggard moment upon his feet. Hanp stirs him roughly with his boot.

Straining and stretching elegantly, with the grace of cats, face over shoulder, this casualty—like a sleepy bed-cramped mistress—responds to the boot's brutal caress.

'Come, you fool Arghol, and eat!'

'Are you there?'

'Have your supper.'

'Is that you?'

'Get up now! It is time.'

'It is you then?'

'I have cooked the food.'

'I am not hungry.'

'It is ready for you. Get up and come in.'

Hanp walks back to the open hut. He leaves Arghol writhing, where he has been sleeping. Hanp exits, with a young bark of precocious catarrh. But Arghol remains upon the ground, his face turned up to the expanse of stellar electricity, his hands pressed upon his ribs in cataplasms, his arms compressed in a bent convex cross. So the chief player lies for a goodish spell, upon the lonely moonlit catasta. This new piece of uncalled-for footballing, upon the part of a brother bondman, has dropped him back into a sort of infant-lethargy. So he crouches with his glazed eyeballs responding to the frosty blankness, self-hugged in pitiful half-slumber.

But soon Arghol rolls about upon his face and, kneeling first, comes to stand upright, firmly and well, stretches and shudders, and passes over to the hut, in the entrance of which Hanp has come out to observe him, his mouth full of black bread. Putting his hand upon Hanp's shoulder, who scowls as the hand touches him, he kisses this fellow-servant upon the cheek. Hanp shakes him off with fury, black bread gushing from his mouth, and passes abruptly inside the hut.

Bastard violence of his half-disciple (métis of an apache of the icy steppe, of sleek citizen, and of his own dumbfounding soul).

His salute was but a symbol, as is a blow from a jackboot! But it has been taken as if it had been the latter, by this churl to whom the lip is more charged with insult than is the toe-cap. (As, mimicking anger, the player in the second role turns from his principal in fierce aversion, he is seen to disinfect his mask, where the salute is supposed to have descended.)

Arghol blocks the doorway now, as he moves in, and stands considering for a series of thick-footed seconds—time advances, but he stands still. As far as time goes, he now goes back. Stationary, with his back to us, he revolves in his mind, he rehearses the nature of the nightly commerce in which we, as spectators, must now prepare to participate. Upon the model of other conversations that have gone before, we should expect what he now in this pausing broods upon.

Every day, after nightfall, hot words have pounded his eardrum, in futile passion of speech. Volleys of abuse, volleys of questions. What did this action mean, what did that action mean? Why this—why that? Nightly the groping fingers of this vulgar intruder have strummed the toppling byzantine organ of his mind. Black fugues resulted—resounding down the Ewigkeit. As he pauses in the entrance, the whole air is shaken by the discords of this vandal hand. Shall he or not bar the barbarian from him for the future? Shall he go in now and deny him all rejoinder? Shall he disallow this mockery of organic speech? But shall he—he was half a mind!

All that is in the hut beneath, he now shuts in, muffled and occulted. The hollow howl of Hanp comes through—

'Come on, you fool. Don't stand moaning in that doorway, come in for mercy's sake! Here is your soup. I have begun.'

'I recognize that I am late.'

'One would say you were tanked—can't you stand up? Come in, don't stagger there and roll your eyes!'

'Oh yes.'

'Sit down, you great green cissy!'

'Yes I will.'

'Yes do!'

(*Arghol steps up to the table slowly, which is just within the door, shading his eye with his hand against the light from the hurricane lamp.*)

'Well,' *he says, and drags the table to the opening of the hut, where the sky light can fall upon the board.* 'Thanks. I was stiff.'

'Stiff! So was I. I am stiff too.'

'I am particularly stiff this evening.'

'More fool you! That is your funeral!'

Harsh bayadere-shepherdess of Pamir—with her Chinese beauty—living on from month to month, in utmost tent, with a steppe-gypsy, a stolid vagrant, lean and lewd—big-boned and big-gristled, red and precocious. The heavy black odour of vast Manchurian garden-deserts, and the disreputable muddy gold squandered by the unknown sun of the Amur, impregnate, placid and massive, the big yellow body-for-sale, which has rolled from the orient—summon those images, to fatten this solitary encounter of the two ill-assorted fellow workmen in the hut. The mind of the one had been thrown open to the other—who had laid violent hands upon what he had found. (This was that mind's one cold flirtation, then cold love.) Excelling in beauty—marked out for Hindu fate of sovereign prostitution, but self-banished out of 'the century'; under a binding vow never to go back to marry or be given in marriage, to love or to hate.

Here, whence he had started, he had come back to rest. Hanp, out-of-work unpaid apprentice, working for his relative, had been thrust upon him as a mate, so circumstances had decided—he had succumbed. Hideous and stupid, this was the masculine, the rough stuff of the fecund horde of men—wand-like phallic cataract poured incessantly into God. The pip of this icy spray, hitting him in the mouth as it flew up, he had tasted with a novel relish—before spitting it out next moment, to such a palate too bitterly uncouth for long.

But to be spat back among men! The other had foreseen this destiny, at the hands of so incalculable a friend. He took the view that such was a poor bargain—he withheld his love, or always if he felt it developing put hatred in its place, not to betray his kind.

THE DIALOGUE BEGINS

The two workers eat their supper at the door of the cabin. Afterwards they sit staring up at the massive ceiling of the star-spangled cupola, surmounting their Bear Pit, their Round O. A long time elapses—in wandering spacious silence. Moving very little except for the slow mechanical revolutions of their heads, they remain with upturned masks. Then Hanp puts his face down and breaks the silence, with a fierce and railing enquiry. The dialogue begins.

HANP. How was it—bad tonight I guess? (*a question that was repeated often*).

ARGHOL. Bad?

HANP. Ay, bad, was it not pretty rotten, eh, old brother? Baddish this evening, was it not?

> (*Arghol lies silent—his hands a thick shell fitting the bombilaton of his outsize head—his face grey vegetable cave.*)

HANP. I heard the bastard—I heard him kicking you. I thought you would be done in this time, straight I did!

ARGHOL. Were you with Hotshepsot?

HANP. A pretty relative! I'd wring the bastard's ugly neck, that's what I would have done six months back! Cannot you bump him off the mad swine?

ARGHOL. No.

HANP. What are hands given you for?

ARGHOL. I cannot guess.

HANP. It's about all a bastard's got, I guess!

ARGHOL. Do you think so?

HANP. Can't you make use of them—you are big enough—you could knock the spunk out of him inside a minute! Smash his great ugly jaw for him, I know I would!

ARGHOL. No.

HANP (*jeering*). *Mote and speck—the universe illimitable*—I know what you'll say! Yes it is true he is a speck. But all of us are specks, all men are specks.

ARGHOL. All men are specks. Spatially specks. Just guts and bones—a little bag. What then?

HANP. To you he is immense!

ARGHOL. No. He is not.

HANP. I say he is!

ARGHOL. Why no. You are quite wrong.

HANP. Oh I say—'You are quite wrong'! We are toffs, aren't we, what!

ARGHOL. I do not see him—he occupies no space to speak of.

HANP (*in a violent snarl*). None—when he kicks you sense-less! You do not see him! But you feel him, don't you, what?

> (*They sit, two grubby shadows, unvaccinated as yet by the moon's lymph—sickened by the immense vague infections of the night.*)

ARGHOL. Well I see how it must look to you. But I have explained—how many times?—Here I get routine.

HANP. Routine! You make me laugh—routine!

ARGHOL. A routine—that is it.

HANP. A routine of assault and battery! What a routine!

ARGHOL. Of course. But the will of the universe is mani-fested, with directness and with persistence.

HANP. With persistence is right.

ARGHOL. Naturally, it is very persistent. That is its will you see.

HANP. Oh ah! Is that its will then? I did not know. I am not in its secrets.

ARGHOL. Nor am I.—It is self-evident though.

HANP. To you it is evident. It's wonderful all the things you see. Am I in the plot? I shouldn't be surprised if I was.

ARGHOL. I dare say you are.

HANP. I shouldn't like to be left out.

> (*There is a pause, in which they turn their faces up to the boundaries of space and stare at the crowds of lights dotting the stellar sea.*)

ARGHOL. Figures of persecution are accidents or adventures for some.

HANP. You have an accident a day of that sort, old fruit!

ARGHOL. Accidents, all the same, however often repeated.

HANP. Oh! Is the sun rising in the morning an accident as well?

ARGHOL. Certainly. There is nothing whatever to show that that is not a simple accident.

HANP. It has happened for a good many years, hasn't it?

ARGHOL. That makes no difference. We have no proof that it will occur again.

HANP. So argue Tom-of-Bedlams and all crackpots.

ARGHOL. No, I am not a victim of the Vultures of the Mind. It was Common Sense that you were hearing.

HANP. And then we wake up!—I know I am ignorant.

ARGHOL. You ask me, and I answer you. That is fair enough. And I tell you these are accidents.

HANP. Bad accidents—just so—nothing more—just con-tree-temps! It is as if you were run over every day at six o'clock, in the same spot.

ARGHOL. Exactly—that is it. That is a good description. That is what happens.

HANP. But why keep the tryst? Why stop where you know you will be knocked down?

ARGHOL. Ah! That is more difficult to satisfy you about I agree.

HANP. Or why not, seeing you can, knock down him who knocks you down?

ARGHOL. To kill, always to kill. It forever comes back to why not to kill. This would have to be a kill.

HANP. Why not? To be killed or to kill—if it is that!

ARGHOL. I understand you. To prick the heart, a pea hardly much more, just under its soft jacket of skin—one prick, I agree, and the bubble pops. There is an end of the matter. That of course is easy. In my case that would be no use at all.

HANP. A lot of use, it seems to me.

ARGHOL. No. No use.

HANP. I know—your usual answer—cut it out! With you it is necessity. You were born to be beaten.

ARGHOL. Put it that way if it helps you to see. Why not?

HANP. I know what your theory is. But what is 'necessity'?

ARGHOL. It is not an accident.

HANP. Oh—now it is not an accident.

ARGHOL. It is an accident that is willed.

HANP. Oh yes—it is done on purpose! At least there you are talking sense. It is done on purpose right enough.

(*Two small black flames, wavering, as their tongues move, drumming out thought, with low earth-draughts and hard sudden winds—dropped like slapping birds from climaxes in the clouds.—No super lens would have dragged them from the key of vastness—they must be severe midgets—brain-specks to the vertiginous vertebrae, slowly-living lines of landscape.*)

ARGHOL. Self, sacred act of violence, is like murder on my face and hands. The stain will not come out.

(*Arghol wrings his hands as if they had been wet.*)

HANP. Self—self! You're right there, your excellency!

ARGHOL. That is the one piece of property all communities have agreed it is illegal to possess. The sweetest-tempered person, once he discovers that you are that sort of criminal, changes his tune—looks askance at you, is upon his guard. When mankind are unable to overcome a personality, they have an immemorial way out of the difficulty. They become it. They imitate and assimilate that Ego until it is no longer one—that is what is called success. As between Personality and the Group, it is forever a question of dog and cat. These two are diametrically opposed species. Self is the ancient race, the rest are the new one. Self is the race that lost. But Mankind still suspects Egotistic plots, and hunts Pretenders!—You are of the upstart fashion.

HANP. Thank you for nothing.

ARGHOL. You egg me on to do in this 'vermin,' as you call our boss, my uncle.

HANP. I say you are mad to put up with it.

ARGHOL. You say 'kill him.' It would be foolish to kill him however.

HANP. I would be a fool, sooner than be kicked to death.

ARGHOL. I don't know. He is very little of a relation.

HANP. What?

ARGHOL. He is only a half-uncle.

HANP. What difference does that make?

ARGHOL. Nothing. He is a sample you understand.

HANP. A nice sample.

ARGHOL. That is as may be. He is as it were an acid advertisement slipped in at the letter-box. The store-rooms of Space, of Time, are dense with frivolous originals.—Then I am used to him, as well.

HANP. You must be by this time.

ARGHOL. I think so.

HANP. I give you that—you are getting into his ways is what you mean. Indeed you must, it could not be otherwise.

ARGHOL. Yes, I can see how my reasoning must seem to you obscure. But there it is. I am that I am. No progress is possible from that.

HANP. So you cannot change anything. I pity you!

ARGHOL. Change is an illusion.

HANP. But so is everything, you say.

ARGHOL. I did not say everything.

HANP. Yes, you have said that to me.

(*The voice of Arghol has none of the sing-song modulations of argument, but has been flat and tired at first—it started to pick up and handle words numbly, like tired compositor. But words have acted upon it as rain upon a plant. His body has taken on a stormy neat brilliance in these soft showers of vocables, he is growing strong as he goes on. At first his arms have been crossed upon his body, to contain mechanically his painful ribs, while he rocks up and down. But now one hand has come off his trunk, and has been slowly waving as he speaks.*

So now one of the two black flames balances giddily erect, whereas the other larger one swerves and sings with speech coldly before it.

Hanp and his master lie in a pool of bleak brown shadow, disturbed once by a rat's plunging head. It rattles forward yet appears to slide upon oiled planes. Arghol shifts his legs out of its path without giving it more attention. Hanp flings a knife after it—you hear the blade strike upon the iron side of stove.

Beyond the canal, brute-lands, shuttered with stony clouds, lie in heavy angles of black sand. They are squirted upon by twenty ragged streams; legions of quails hop parasitically within the miniature cliffs. The uncle of Arghol is the local wheelwright, upon the extremities of this small city. Two hundred miles to the north the Arctic circle sweeps. Sinister tramps, its winds come wandering down the highway, fatigued and chill, doors shut against them as they come snooping round the homesteads of dark pine.)

ARGHOL. First—to begin where all is at its simplest. (*He elevates pontifically his right-hand index finger, his long nail gilded with a cracked earthy impasto.*) Lily pollen of Ideal upon red badge of our predatory category. (*He draws in a breath, as if inhaling a mighty shadow, and sweeps mesmerically a powerful and dejected hand.*) Scrape off—scrape off or worse wear down, this nap of sentiment—and behold you will have lost your appetite. Obviously—it is the pretty coating does allow us that. That even you must be able to conjecture. But, for my own part, I never happen to have wished, in any case, to devour Robinson, or to make a square meal off Smith. Smith, he is tough, Robinson dull and unpalatable—both are distasteful to me in a word. So perhaps I am too vain to do an injury. It may well be I am too superb ever to lift a finger when I am assailed—you have my permission to say that if you care to. A man eats his lamb chop, forgetting it is his gentle neighbour; he drinks when he makes merry, a symbolic blood, of a divinity that has been done to death; and in his domestic joss-house gossips, of an evening, of the latest version of his god, as canvassed in his newspaper.

HANP (*growling in his corner*). We can't all be gentlemen. We can't all be fine gentlemen!

ARGHOL (*in a dull roar of surprise*). Why should we wish to be that in God's name, I don't understand you, Hanp!

HANP. No nor yet vegetarians—turning up our noses at lamb.

ARGHOL (*mournfully*). Why vegetarian? The vegetarian is no gentleman.

HANP. No? I didn't know. I thought he was for sure.

ARGHOL. Certainly not. There you are quite wrong.

HANP. Go on! Isn't he one? I made sure he was.

ARGHOL. By no means. Decidedly not. Gentleman and vegetarian should never be mentioned in the same breath.

HANP. I'm sure I'm very sorry, milord, if I mentioned!

ARGHOL. Why?

HANP. I'm only a poor peasant lad. Let me down light! I know no better.

ARGHOL. You are too modest. You have practically all the instincts of a gentleman. Do not allow yourself to be intimidated by the word. A mere blood-stained shibboleth.

HANP. Blood-stained—go on, is that right! I didn't know. Am I one? Why that's news to me.

ARGHOL. Of course you are. You have all the instincts. You are typical, I would go so far as to say that.

HANP. No would you straight—you do surprise me! I'm getting conceited you know, you'd better be careful—I'm not used to compliments.

ARGHOL. Yes. I don't mean nature's gentleman either.

HANP. Don't you—is that a fact?

ARGHOL. No—nothing ambiguous of that sort.

HANP. Nothing what?

ARGHOL. I meant what I said first—you are the real thing.

HANP. Oh you did, did you! I am pleased to hear you meant it—thank you for nothing, my lord Sark!

ARGHOL. You are mistaken, I am not Sark. And don't thank me.

HANP. No? I thought I ought to. P'r'aps I should.

ARGHOL. Certainly not—I am not responsible for you.

HANP. Carry on! Carry on!—still yours is a hard lot, Argie-boy—we must let you have your little joke I guess, it gives you pleasure, and it don't hurt me.

ARGHOL. Shall I continue then?

HANP. Yes whoop me up—I feel in need of it.

ARGHOL. Well then—I go back to the simplest things of all.

HANP. That's right—they cannot be too simple for the likes of me.

(Arghol sights on to him, along his outstretched arm, then, throwing his hands up into the air, he falls back heavily in a rushing collapse, pillowed by forearms—brawn glued on brawn, a pneumatic furrow—which in his fall he has flung behind him, beneath his rolling headpiece, which at length comes to rest, after rocking to and fro a little, and he commences speaking.)

ARGHOL. Have you ever heard the answer made by Jim Crow to Jack Frost—when asked by Jack why his skin was black like night?

HANP (*with a rumble of suspicion*). Well what did Jim say?

ARGHOL. Why Jim said the day, where he came from, was looked down upon. It was treated as a disturbance of the natural order. It was the night as it were that was the true daytime. His skin conformed to the true canon. He was the normal fellow—it was Jack Frost was eccentric with his white countenance.

HANP. Well, Arghol, and what do you want me to understand by your Jim Crow and your Jack Frost?

ARGHOL. Scratch any of us, and our whiteness is seen to be skin-deep—Jim Crow is right, that is the moral. Lily pollen of Ideal! The wild machine—that is the animal—alone is normal. And that is the Dark Night of the Body—with apologies to Jack of the Cross!

HANP. Who's that whose pardon you're asking?

ARGHOL. No one, a dago.

HANP. Was that Jack Crow?

(Arghol sits up. He crosses his legs and underpins himself

*with a big chopping-block, which he rolls forward. It is
the height of a substantial keg. He picks up a cleaver, and
surveys its edge. He puts it down, and props himself upon
the chopping-block property, just where the chicken got
the chopper, and droops to his right hand to speak into
the earth.)*

ARGHOL. I will make it my best endeavour to show you
where you stand. Can I speak more fairly than that?

HANP. Where *you* stand, I think you mean.

ARGHOL. We say that we exist. What does that signify,
except a meaningless battle of parts? And what may the nature
be of the intelligent Whole—is it even intelligent? As for us. Is
it to exist at all to be such wretched fractions as we are? I lean
upon this chopping-block, where you have decapitated a fowl.
When you cut into fragments a chicken, the piece cut off does
not make up a smaller chicken, does it, but only a dead particle.
We are such particles. Is the cosmic bird alive, and still intact,
or is it beheaded and does it run headlong in an automatic
death-sprint, nowhere in particular—having at some earlier
period received the coup de grâce? Is something of that sort
what is occurring, and is that what we misname life?

HANP. Answer your own questions, Mr Philosopher.—I give
it up!

ARGHOL. Existence. Loud feeble sunset—blaring like lumpish, savage clown, alive with rigid tinsel, tricked out in louse-
infested pantaloons, before a misty entrance, upon the trestled
balcony of a marquee, announcing events in a stale programme
of a thousand breakneck sports—of poodles that sit up to tea,
and of handcuffed men who eat their food or paint a landscape with the sole assistance of their feet—promising laughter
and death mixed—of fat-bottomed pantomimes and mortal
accidents from trapezes in the roof—the pink-tighted flesh of
the female and the frisking beneath it of a milk-white horse-
flesh to delight the horsy, punctuated throughout with the
chatter of skilled Fools: a showman who bellows down to
penniless herds, their eyes red with stupidity, crowding beneath
him clutching their sixpences.

*(Hanp snorts at the 'penniless herds'—his bust is out of
the picture but he can be heard to scratch his head and
to expectorate.)*

ARGHOL. And after that? There must be an after-that to

such a description?—To leave violently this slow monotonous life; that is, to take header into the boiling starry cold. (For with me some guilty fire of friction, unspent in solitariness, will reach the utmost constellations.) Hell of those Heavens uncovered, whirling pit, every evening! You cling to any object, dig your nails into the galloping terra firma beneath you, not to drop into it.

(Timber merchants in a big way are the next neighbours of the ancient figure-yard. As if it were their garden, a pine wood springs up among their godowns packed with timber. Now the powerful night plunges its electric arms down into the fir-garden. Beyond the red-rimmed doorway of the hut are the big Christmas trees. Giddy and expanding in drunken walls, the drastic beams of the thick white night shift, cross, and in places go opaque, in iceberg fashion, into slab, shaft or cube. So ice for the starlight, silver for sand, and the black boxes of the frame-dwellings or sheds, and black for the big Christmas bushes.

Ponderous arabesques of red cloud, nothing but that, are visible to Arghol. The lines of the red cumulus do not terminate at the door's frame, but press on into the shadows within the hut, in tyrannous continuity. As a cloud drives eastward, out of this framework, its weight passes, with spiritual menace, into the hut. A thunderous atmosphere thickens about the heads of the two performers. Investment of the red universe! The hut is a vortex, it is only too plain, and into its dark mouth all that is in movement in the visible world tends to be engulfed.

Arghol is paler, he tosses clumsily and swiftly from side to side, as if he were asleep. He thrusts his body out into the yard. The face of Hanp appears within the opening.—Now the clouds it seems have room to waste themselves. The land continues, in dull form, one per cent animal, these immense bird-amœbas. The earth pulses up against his side and reverberates. He drags hot palms along the surface of the ground, caressing its explosive harshness.

The aloof master of this arc-lit vortex is Arghol. His mask has been designed to represent this magical function. So it responds, calm seismograph of eruptions in the heavens, to the transformations of the glittering spiral—of this telescopic, scenographic, man-pit of a proscenium—arranged as a stage might be in Arcturus, if the spectators were to be persons on the Earth.

But abruptly everything flicks out. There is a moment of complete eclipse—it is as if there had been a short-circuit. In the momentary blank a close-up of the chief player's head is conveyed, in a breathless upward rush, to the most distant watchers and far-seated listeners-in. By mechanical enlargement, as it lolls without the hatchway, where the action is proceeding, it is snatched up to be scrutinized by the busybodies in the remotest galleries of Time. First, out of the abyss, there is the rapid approach of a dark and massive object: then the face stands out for all! to see—a pallid mask, but its mouth in mechanical movement, like that of a fish, brought up for an instant to gasp in a distant element. All gaze upon it as upon a spectacle of awe.

A black and herculean, a bearded Ashtarte—epicene divinity of an iron tribe of spartan habit, of in part subarctic habitat, and in part of less high latitudes—hyperbarbarous of course and entirely protohistorical. Everyone sees at once the Tundra in these lineaments—everybody detects the contact with those caravans that linked Sumeria or the Indus with Cathay. Lofty tents, sonorous with October rains, swarming from vast bright doll-like asiatic lakes. The faces of the mechanical nomads, following the tracks of stars in the mirrors of the dark-blue watercourses, until sea-struck, all the reflections of the advancing masks smashed up—thundering engine of red water! There was the pink idle brotherhood of the small stars as well, passed over by rough cloud of sea.

But cataclysm of premature decadence—it is the débâcle! Extermination from within of the resounding, sombre, summer-tents. Within a decade no more, all is obliterated, which is strictly human. But left behind is a dark assemblage of furious images, crowds of chimeras—upright among the rotting tents, beneath the clouds of vultures—left to confront the invader, as with many dubious halts he steals up to discover what disaster has overtaken this great military people. An immense production of barren muscular girl idols—wood, verdigris, jade and copper, desert-pigments called in to complicate, with even the pelts of quadrupeds and plumage of polar waterfowl. A hundred idols per head of the population—or each male tribesman encumbered with a harem of a hundred wooden or stone succubuses. Plainly a race swamped in a hurricane of art—descending upon the high narrow and unsheltered souls of its fanatical master-craftsmen and idolatrous priests in one.

This was the gist of the book-of-words, sketched out to accompany the close-up of the exotic headpiece of Arghol—a headpiece heavy and bird-like, weighted with a ballast of pig-iron to strike with—living enchained upon his mobile body— ungainly red atlantic wave!

But SHATTER this pullulation that has been released to assist the vision—dam up these images!—the order goes out. Forthwith the close-upped headpiece drops like a thunderbolt, down into its socket again—the starlit catasta—to its allotted station in the Play. It is observed to be lolling as before, a short span without the black hatchway, where it bellows its part beneath the cataract of stars!

Hanp sees the spark, as he thinks, burning less brightly in this brazier of proud discourse in front of him, and so seeks to blow upon it—a little quietly—in a manner calculated to revive its flame.)

HANP. To have read all the books of the great cities Arghol — and to come back here to take up this life again—such a life as this!

> (*Coaxing—genuine stupefaction—reproach, perhaps a trap.*)

ARGHOL. I know. But I have answered that.

> (*The master lifts up his expensively carved head once more, and he precedes the false disciple through the giant furnitures of his consciousness—cold, unbenevolent—perpetual inspector of himself. Doors open upon noisy blankness. Garrets gape like the skeletons of shipwrecked galleons. A shout down a passage, to demonstrate its extent—as it were a horizontal well, the voice coming back with unexpectedness of expert pugilistics.*)

ARGHOL. I must live, like a tree, there where I grow! An inch to left or right would be too much! In the town I felt unrighteous, for I was escaping from the blows—the home-anger—destiny of here! Fate planted me in this identical soil, that I should suffer at the hands of this very person.

HANP. At the feet you mean—at the feet!

ARGHOL. It was I that was meant! It is no use disguising it. It was I who was intended—no other square peg would fit this square hole, nor I any other!

HANP. A lot of hard thinking was done when you were born and that's a fact!

ARGHOL. No thinking at all.

HANP. God helps those who help themselves, they say.

ARGHOL. Selfishness, flouting of destiny, it has seemed to me—to step so much as an inch out of the bull's eye of one's birth. When it is obviously a bull's eye!

HANP. As it is here right enough—a bloody target!

ARGHOL. A visionary tree. Not migratory. Visions from within—that is the idea of it. A man with a headache lies in deliberate leaden inanimation—he isolates his body, floods it with phlegm, sucks numbness up into his brain. So it should be with the spirit, maybe. Soul is a good sodden word, of the old verbal dough. Use that—say soul. A soul, that is the wettest dough, the doughiest plumber's stock-in-trade. It is the perfect bullet. To drop down Eternity like a plummet—accumulate in myself, day after day, a dense concentration of pig life! Nothing spent, stored rather in strong stagnation, till rid at last of the evaporation and lightness characteristic of men! Thus to burst Death's membrane through—slog beyond—not float in appalling distances!

(Arghol stares back at the glittering heavens, and waves his hand, palm upward, thumb depressed.)

ARGHOL: Energy has been fastened upon me from nowhere—heavy, astonished, resigned, I accept it. It is without meaning I agree—or at least if it have a meaning I cannot discern it. However, I will use it, as a prisoner his sheet or bedding for escape. Not as a means of idle humiliation. Why should I not make use of these senseless gifts? One night Death left his card. I was not familiar with the name he chose, but the black mourning edge was deep. I flung it back. A thousand awakenings of violence visited me then. I was ready to act—for a moment I was a stimulus-response machine which would have elicited your admiration. And all for death!

HANP *(exposing his ragged teeth in a brief croak of laughter)*. I wish I'd seen you then!

ARGHOL. Indeed I wish you had. For once I was your man! Next day, as my mad relative as usual came at me, gurgling and kicking, I had a jack-knife up my sleeve—ready for all those actions that you recommend.

HANP. What happened then?

ARGHOL. Why nothing I'm afraid. I cut myself instead—he drove the knife point into the flesh of my arm. The first kick brought me to my senses.

HANP. How?

ARGHOL. I saw the matter in a clear light at once. No, it is no use. Besides, a superstition—a habit—is there, curbing him mathematically: that of not killing me. I am quite safe really in his hands. I should know an ounce of effort more.—See how he loads my plate! He wishes me to be alive.

(A hawker who is but a languid kestrel, a sparrow-hawk in fact of a work-shy street-hawker—propelling his handcart, seesawing upon its axle, with a doldrum-shuffle—his upper half sprawled in its stern-sheets, a cargo of sodden sacks depressing its top-heavy prow—a son of the sensational masses, asking nothing better than to park his barrow and umpire a gutter-battle. But in luck's way, when least expecting luck, he runs into an A.1 disturbance. Gulping, he watches this big struggling stiff (with the fire-name of Arghol) through his puffed slits (moist with a tearful pus of continual expectation of trouble). Fate features as the Police Force, in this topsy-turvy mix-up— Fate is the favourite—everybody changes sides, everybody goes over to the Cossacks! For this big rebel has a light of alien heroism in his eyes-that-speak-another-language—black and suspect, by no means a true-blue—there is something even worse than a civic indignation that is ploughing up his high-brow brow! Here is no honest criminal—so, for want of a better champion, why Up the Police! What are these patriot gestures in a row in a back-alley? So Up Fate! shout all and sundry. For Fate to fall upon this declamatory outcast with all its battery of night-sticks and wipe the landscape with him, is what Hanp cries out to see! So egg-on Fate of course!—then egg-on (as best one can) this strange adversary of Law and Order.

Port-prowler first, but like a strayed serf of Cosmopolis, serving the tongue and gait of the metropolitan gutter within the grasp and aroma of the convulsive bitter emptiness of the sea: dry-salted in slow acrid airs—aerian flood not stopped by beach, jetty or cliff, but dying beyond, in dirty warmth of harbour-boulevards. One of the children of an ocean-township, leaned upon by two wild skies—the lower opaque one washes it with noisy clouds, or lies giddily flush with its street-crevices, wedges of ink-black air, flooding its fish-halls and municipal arches with a thick emptiness of dung-red light. It sends ships up through its slight rock of houses, week by week. Stolidly they steam up to its hollow middle. This is a handsome deep green cistern. Big timber boats to about the number of nine-teen—that is nineteen nomad souls for its amphibious carcass—they swim locked within its bulky stone-sided foss, its inner dock—the swimming-bath of the infant Hanp—the big boudoir-mirror of his Hanp-faced mamma, a quayside squatter to attend The Catch, brought in by the local Oedipuses of the pink-bronzed fisher-broods.)

HANP. DEST-TIN-NEE!

ARGHOL. What is it?

HANP. You trot it out your bloody fate-word.

ARGHOL. You are muttering, Hanp. I cannot hear you quite.

HANP. It's fate this and fate that.

ARGHOL. Ah, you are grumbling.

HANP. What is it anyway?

ARGHOL. What of it?—I am deaf on my left side.

(*Hanp crawls forward towards the statue drooping upon the chopping-block, crossly to cross-question—propped up to muffle a malevolent snigger with a wad of crawling finger-joints, his eyes constricted to a somnolent squint.*)

HANP. Nelson's blind eye—and the held-up telescope, against the Dutch!

ARGHOL. No—I got it badly on the left tonight. I am numb all the way up and deaf as a post. Only on that side.

HANP. Well go on. I know you want to get it off your chest! Carry on with it, brother.

ARGHOL. What's that? With what?

HANP. You know! All about fate. What is it, Arghol? Strike up, boy! Have I not put the big question? We may as well have it. I'm only a poor Ploughing Peter though—make it easy for us, won't you, boss!

ARGHOL (*morosely regarding the tempter and coaxer*). Destiny. A preordained pattern. A pattern that is consistent with itself.

HANP. Oh: pattern. If someone asked me I should answer *pattern*, should I, when they said What's fate?

(*Hanp drags himself a little nearer, squinting more, showing a smallish, well-turned tusk.*)

HANP. I can say fate, that's just as good: 'fate's' easier, is that O.K.?

ARGHOL. It doesn't matter.

HANP. How can it be your fate to stop round here—I ask you? It isn't reasonable. You're a philosopher—what you do must be reasonable too.

ARGHOL. That does not follow. But why not be here—as much as there? I don't see that that presents any difficulty.

HANP. But why more than go back and live in the city? Why more here than there?

ARGHOL. It happens like that. I am here.

HANP. Or to cross to America?

ARGHOL. America!

HANP. What's the matter with that? New York! That's a better place than this, isn't it? You have the money.

ARGHOL. Geography does not interest me. America is geography. All those things are maps no more.

HANP. It's the map of a fine country is America. It is a free country, that's something.

ARGHOL. 'Free'—that is a mistake.

HANP. Americans are freer than us!

ARGHOL. Free to do what? That is the point. Free means just nothing.

HANP. I wish I was there, that's all! Let me get the chance, I'd hop it tonight.

ARGHOL. You would find it just the same. Those days are past, as well. Go West is the injunction of a distant yesterday.

HANP. You would chain us all down like trees! At least a man has not the status of a dog across the ocean—here our sort are the latter, dogs. I would go if I had the cash tomorrow.

ARGHOL. You'd be a fool—you'd lose your cash and get nothing for it. Better to stop where you are and keep your cash.

HANP. You would stop here, spouting all by yourself, about your bloody stars, we know that, till doomsday.

ARGHOL. How do you picture to yourself New York? I have explained to you what all great towns are like. All cities are imitations of American. There is no need to go there to be in America. Any city's just the same.

HANP. All the more reason to go there. If that is the model for the rest. It is a New World. That's what they call it—New World!

ARGHOL. They call it—yes. There is no 'new world'—those are just words.

HANP. None so you say, but there is a new world—in fact, not in the name only. Yours are words too, if it comes to that.

ARGHOL. There is nothing new there. Your heaven across the waves is an affair of a few high buildings—big plants, Big Business. You'd find out your mistake soon enough—you'd live much as you do here—worse, in fact. Believe it or not, there is no way out! There is no 'new' anything. Offences against the discipline of the universe are registered by a sort of conscience—prior to the kicks. For instance, blows rain upon me here—mine is not a popular post, far from it. It is my destiny. There is no new world at all events for me.

HANP. What a destiny!

ARGHOL. Certainly not an agreeable one.

HANP. There I shall not contradict you!

ARGHOL. I did not choose it. It is not my idea of a nice destiny.

HANP. That's something, anyway—if it was! But how can it be the fate of a man as clever as you to live buried in this lousy hole, except from choice. You are mad, that's what it is.

ARGHOL. Ah, how. Do not ask me that—I am in the dark as much as you! I simply cannot understand it. When I look round, I am sometimes dumbfounded at the oddness, more than you! I am disgusted too. I am disgusted with myself for being guilty of such a destiny—and such a décor! I am ashamed of absolutely everything—to be perfectly frank.

HANP. That you put on—you know you put that on! You have done the whole thing yourself from start to finish!

ARGHOL. I! What have I done?

HANP. Mounted the whole bag of tricks from top to bottom —made the bed you were to lie on with your eyes open!

ARGHOL. The bed!

HANP. You understand me very well. You are foxing—it's no use throwing up your hands!

ARGHOL. No, I don't understand you. You are a peculiar person. I do not understand.

HANP. All is your doing. You came down here—did he not meet you hat in hand? Hotshepsot tried to sleep with you— you had fish for breakfast—you had the best bed in the house. And what happened? You forced that bastard to ill-use you.

Yes you did! You struck the first blow yourself—at yourself I
might almost say. You made him knock you about—you asked
to be cuffed and kicked—I saw you doing it. Then you made
him do it harder. Even then for you (for about that you were
particular) it was not hard enough! Yes, you even caused him
to kick you at an appointed time—at a set place! Am I not
speaking the truth? You have trained him like a performing
dog. He is as scared of you as hell—you know that is the truth!
Deny it if you can! But it doesn't matter if you do!

(*Arghol draws away from Hanp, his eyes somewhat
dilated, as if in an absent-minded fit of half-suppressed
alarm. Flinging his arms up he yawns in big mechanical
spasms, and then gets up upon the chopping-block—
sitting with his hands in his lap and his back thrust
against the jamb of the hut.*)

HANP. Is it not true, what I have just said? Word for word.
What is your answer?

ARGHOL. It is your view of me. It is how you interpret
this. But if what you said were true, it would still be my fate,
as you wish us to call it.

HANP. Not unless you are fate! You are not that, are you?

ARGHOL. In a sense I agree with you. I am.

HANP. Oh well, if you are destiny, we then know where we
stand—you talk a lot about yourself—that ends the argument!

ARGHOL (*in a strong piping wail*). Our soul is wild, with
primitiveness of its own. Its wilderness is anywhere—in a shop,
sailing, reading psalms. Anything I possess is drunk up here
upon the world's brink, by big stars, and returned me in the
shape of thought, ponderous as a meteorite. The stone of the
stars will serve for my seal and emblem. I practise with it a
monotonous 'putting,' so that I may hit Death when he comes.

HANP. Yes, it is a strange game you play here all right, all
on your own—at the back of beyond, in the purlieus of the
great Nothing, as you call it! No one can deny that. But as to
the thought you boast about, what is the use of it? It is wasted
in this wilderness—wilderness, that is the word! It is a bloody
wilderness.

ARGHOL. A thought weighs less in a million brains than in
one. No one is conjuror enough to prevent spilling—rather, the
bastard form infects the original. Famous men are those who
have exchanged themselves against a thousand idiots—when

you hear that a famous man has died penniless and diseased, you say—'Well served!' He has brought it upon himself! Part of life's plan is that the best among us if they are not careful become those cheap scarecrows. All life-on-earth is contingent upon such blurred conditions—there is exemption for no one. The penalty is methodic degradation. Sacrifice of the original solitude of man's ego is the price exacted. There is no help for it—every gesture and syllable goes to the integration of that universal fate. Already the child has soiled himself beyond recognition. Accept it or not, that is the law—Anything but yourself is dirt. Anybody, that is. All people, in their outer contacts, are unclean. If you asked me why I lived at all I could only reply that it was because I do not feel clean enough to enter upon my pompes funèbres and kick the bucket. To make it worth while to destroy myself, there is not enough of myself there to do it with and that's a fact!

(*A laugh, packed with all the most crackling vibrations of a vicious hatred—not hoping to carry—snapped like a fiddle-string in the middle.*)

HANP. Sour grapes! That's about the size of it, milord! And so you let yourself be kicked to death here out of spite, that's your account of the matter! Why, perhaps it is not you who is kicked at all!

ARGHOL. Indeed perhaps it is not.

HOTSHEPSOT. Well take that! See if that's you or not!

(*While this dialogue has been proceeding, Hotshepsot has come across the yard, first appearing above the opal cloudlet, from the direction of the canal. She is a big girl with a big roll in the hips and carrying her head erect and without movement in contrast to her revolving middle, as if it had been used to oriental pitchers and the desert palm wells. She has ear-rings of beaten gold.*

As Hotshepsot says take that! *she strikes Arghol heavily across the mouth with a thick white fist with divers rings. He remains with his head pushed up against the bulging jamb of the hut door and his hands do not leave his lap—gazing at her with a steady and confirmed surprise.*)

HOTSHEPSOT. I've seen your sort before!

ARGHOL. Where, Hotshepsot? What sort, Hotshepsot?

HOTSHEPSOT. I'll show you where!

(Seizing a convenient spoke, Hotshepsot whirls it in the starlit air and brings it down upon his head. Arghol falls off the chopping-block as if poleaxed, in the direction of the woman, and lies at full length in the ex-figure-yard, face down, inert.)

HOTSHEPSOT. Keeping this boy out of bed, to listen to your mad talk—great loud-tongued cissy-man—night after night! What do you want with him, eh, Mister Palaver? What is he to you? He must want something to do to listen to your great moony clapper, I should say!

HANP. Cut it out, Hotshepsot!

HOTSHEPSOT. He's shamming dead. I'll teach him to lie doggo!

(Hotshepsot catches sight of the cleaver, which is lying just within the door of the hut. She seizes it, upon the ground, and flourishing it in her uplifted hand, is turning to make a rush at Arghol when Hanp trips her up. With a roaring scream Hotshepsot disappears head-first down the companion-ladder that leads to the mimes' quarters. The last thing that is seen of her is the kicking pair of fleshy knees, and an umbrella of billowing peasant petticoats, like a parachute that fills with wind. Her bumpings can be numbered. The uproar of her descent dies down.)

HANP *(sitting up)*. She-cat! What business is it of hers, I'd like to know!

(Arghol sits up—in an impenetrable stare he focuses his fellow-workman. Rolling abruptly upon his right hip—with the dexterity of a particularly active beggar-cripple—he crawls back to the chopping-block, over which he throws his arm. Then he swings his face up to the sky, as if to interrogate the thousands of electric sparks above them, to enquire which might be responsible for this last contretemps. His eyes come to rest upon the seven rishis. Their simple structure causes them to be the peace-spot in his planetarium.)

HANP. I suppose you'll say you didn't bring that on yourself!

ARGHOL. It seems to me she did it of her own volition.

(Hanp breaks into a loud bleating peal of hostile laughing, which reverberates in the black shaft at his back, down which Hotshepsot has so abruptly shot.)

HANP. You understand well enough why she did it! Don't make out you don't know that!

ARGHOL. I am at a loss to know why Hotshepsot behaves in that objectionable manner. Is that a natural way in which to behave? It appears to me extremely unusual.

HANP. Very good, Doctor Fox—but how about yours? Curl up your fists in your lap—sit like a sanctimonious punching-ball—who would not have a smack at it for fun and gratis?

ARGHOL. Did I invite that slap on the lips from Hotshep-sot? I did not even see her. She came up from behind.

HANP. Hotshepsot is only human. It wasn't the first she had given you, was it?

ARGHOL. I suppose not. No, not the first. She certainly appears to be contracting the habit.

HANP. Certainly she is—a most unusual habit, wot wot! To break her of it—why you will simply have to lift a finger—to push her away next time! Stick up your finger and poke the girl off—like that!

(*Finically, Hanp extends his index finger, and makes the gesture of compelling some foreign body, of feather-weight importance, to withdraw, or at least keep its beastly distance.*)

ARGHOL. I cannot engage in battle with Miss Hotshepsot.

HANP. But how did she come to form that habit in the first instance? That is what I should like to know.

ARGHOL. Frankly, so should I. It is mysterious. I confess I have not the least idea. I was not paying much attention, I am afraid, at the time.

HANP. No, I'll bet you weren't. Well, I will tell you how—would you like to know? She formed it in the same way that he did!

ARGHOL. Indeed. You think so? That I should rather doubt.

HANP. You can take it from me, that was the way all right! She could not help herself! She's a quiet girl. A little interfering, but quite ladylike. You drove her to it. And you meant to do so too—you're shamming stupid—that's all right!

(*Arghol throws up his hands, in conventional remon-strance, and for the first time smiles at his now flushed accuser. For the moment Hanp says nothing more. Then he gets up from the ground, and moving across to the table, drinks a tumbler of water. Turning round slowly he looks down at Arghol, who is just outside the hut, still squatting against the chopping-block.*)

HANP. Tell me another thing. Have your answer ready!

ARGHOL. What do you mean? An answer ready? Am I not quick enough at what is called the uptake?—Answer!

HANP. Well, tell me—why you talk so much! To me! It is to me! I want to know.

ARGHOL. What do you mean by that?

HANP. All the talking you do does not seem to bear out your pretensions. For what you pretend you are, you talk too much, Mr Arghol—you see what I'm trying to drive at I hope.

ARGHOL. That may be. But why do you make these observations?

HANP. I suppose I have a right to my opinions! I have my thoughts, you know. I ask questions for information. That's all, but please don't trouble.

(Disrespect or mocking, in the hush of the séance, or at the magical conversazione of the Shaman, is succeeded by offended silence, on the part of the common spook or the siberian spiritist. The shy Siberians even will immediately withdraw. A suppressed splutter of nervous mirth is enough. So silence, not visibly offended, ensues, between the chief players, in a long lazy interval. The rustic master—cavernously, centrically, hemicyclically, real—lies back indifferent. His booted feet repose—two massive, fast-shut volumes—under the nose of the lowering disciple. Then Arghol opens his jaws wide once more, in egotistic self-castigation.)

ARGHOL. Again let me do a lot of extraordinary talking. Let me do a lot. Watch me most closely. Trap me in my words —track back the cause in laying hold more securely of the effect. As to the use of my tongue, that is a purgative. But the doctoring admittedly is fouler often than the complaint. Men possess a repulsive deformity, it is generally referred to as 'Myself.' This is a disfiguring disease. Promiscuous rubbing against their fellows is responsible for it. As to the activity you call in question, namely *talking*—why that is just such an unsuitable rubbing and contact too. The routine existence of all men is determined, in its most trivial details, by the requirements of this abominable ailment—namely Self. Only one operation can cure it—the classical stoic operation, namely— emptying an artery into the bath. But Self is enormous—the thing is like a snuffling parasite, far more bulky than the louse or flea. I have smashed it against me. Still, however, the creature writhes, a turbulent mess. I have shrunk it in frosty climates, and attempted to starve it out. But it has filtered filth into me, until my most hermetic solitude is impure as the water of a public washing-brook.

(*This diatribe against something, which he had christened* Self, *focuses the physical repulsion of the disciple. Even as he had prepared Hotshepsot, so this great rhapsodical fellow was preparing him—he was being baited with disgust! The more this Master cancelled in him the satisfactory self-feelings, the more a contemptible matter showed itself, disfiguring the image of the Master—sunken mirror, that gave back Hanp's essential sickly silhouette as Hanp peered in. He hated himself in hating him—such was the magic of this looking-glass, which was at the same time a trap.*

The price of the sharp vision of this arrogant mastery was contamination of the masterful. So Hanp got the breath of his most private Hanpness back from the surface of this treacherously polished intellect.

In this master-spirit too many things inhabited together for true hygiene certainly. Is a single spirit too narrow an abode for genius?—Argument for the Mob! Argument for Mister Nobody!—To have Humanity inside you—is that to keep a doss-house malgré soi? At least upon such a scale, to organize it is not a bagatelle. So those who would, out of hand, disperse these impure monopolies are not so utterly mistaken then? Let everybody get his little bit. Intellectual Balham, rather than intellectual Bedlam! Down with the dirty highbrow Giants!)

ARGHOL. Are those great stars wonder-portions of an absolute, magnitude of magnitudes, or no more than the electric bulbs in the work-shop? We are beneath the coverlet of earth, as to the roots of our essence. Esse is percipi, at least we see —that is all that can be said for us. Our eyes are on a par with the stellar universes. Our brains are sick with the distances achieved by our instruments.—There is a snow-down on that sand hillock, the stars are snowing, do you see it there?

(*Arghol heaves himself up, as if to uproot himself from his gravitational attachments, and looks about him, but begins to stare instead in a blank and astonished fashion at the watchful Hanp, who has meantime dropped upon a bench, and is sprawling upon the table, which occupies*

*all the left hand of the cavity which stands for the within
of the sham-hut.)*

ARGHOL. Why do I wag my tongue, which should be a
dumb gland in your philosophy, and agitate my lips and jaws?
Is that the question before the meeting?

HANP. That's about the size of it, milord.

ARGHOL. It is because the words are addressed to you, you
say—Why to me? That is your question.

HANP. Right again. Where do I come in, a humble labourer?
I'm nobody.

ARGHOL. Why do I talk to Nobody—is that the question
before the meeting now? Well, it is not to you really. It is to
myself. That is the reply.

HANP. Short and sweet. I'm not here in fact at all, as you
put it—you'd push me off the earth in your account of it.

ARGHOL. It was because you were nobody and nothing,
that's the fact. But it is a physical matter too—simply to make
use of one's mouth and stretch one's tongue. My thoughts to
walk abroad—not for ever to be stuffed up in my head—ideas
to banjo this big sounding-box—to pipe with this big windbag
of a body. That is one reason among several.

HANP. You must have a nice time on your own, with your
brass-band and all!

ARGHOL. There was more to it—than that you just were
Nothing though.

HANP. Oh ah, I guessed that wasn't all by a long shot!

ARGHOL. You struck me, to start with, as such a poor dim
Nobody.

HANP. Yes, yes—a dark star as you call them, and one of
The Poor on top of that!

ARGHOL. Such a thrasonic bubble of a boy, blown up from
the rotten suds on a washing-Wednesday by a half-wit mamma—

HANP. I get your meaning perfectly—go on!

ARGHOL. Beneath contempt—a poop fired off by Mother-
Nature in derision, a bad smell—so there was some hope for
you—if you get me, to talk American.

HANP. That's interesting—that's very interesting—I follow
all you say quite well, though on my own I couldn't half think
all that up, being uneducated.

ARGHOL. Be that upon your own head. It is you who have
insisted. I did not ask to say all this.

HANP. Quite so, sir—it's me that is to blame, I quite see that!

ARGHOL. So long as we are not at cross purposes.—From such a character as yours what was there to expect? That clearly is far better, is it not, than mere little painful somethings? You were nothing, or rather that negation, which probably I had always desired to encounter—or just found useful at the present juncture, it might be that.

(Arghol rises to his feet. His hands thrust in his corduroy jacket pockets, he drops against the nearest doorpost, the right-hand one. He gazes with a great solemn unblinking intentness into the face of Hanp, considering the changes of his expression, the coming and going of colour, with the manner of a chemist observing the behaviour of gases in a retort.)

ARGHOL. That is the best that I can do—you have your answer—now chew the cud! I can say more, of course.

HANP. I'll bet you can!

ARGHOL. I am a great extraordinary talking man, who only stops to sleep—my relatives assault me because I will not hold my tongue. I can go on.

HANP. Without asking my leave, I know—why do you stop? Go on!

ARGHOL. I can talk off a *dog's* hind leg!

HANP. Thank you for 'dog'—a great talking-man like you has his tongue—dogs have their teeth!

ARGHOL. My constant discovery is that you are me—a strange thought, what say you, Hanp?

HANP. Peculiar I call it—but go on, sir, what next?

ARGHOL. We are improperly separate. You grow in me. I talk to you for half-an-hour—it requires a good half-hour to effect this, but never more, just thirty minutes by the clock.

HANP. No, go on—is that all?

ARGHOL. As I get warmed up, progressively I become disgusted with myself as I find you in me so much *chez soi*—but more and more!

HANP. No!—more and more!

ARGHOL. I never more, having met you and taken you on board, will be the captain-of-my-soul I was!—While I was talking, a half-minute back, I made a fresh discovery.

HANP. What another one?

ARGHOL. That's it! I find I wished to make of you a yapping

Poodle-parasite, a sort of mechanical bow-wow, to fetch and carry, for my inferior nature—to be The Animal to me! The fact is I shall be a prostitute always—I hope you understand!

HANP. I think I do—I see just what you're aiming at!

ARGHOL. I wished—I've just found out—to make you my self, you see. But every man who wishes that—to make out of another an inferior Self—is lost. He's after a mate for his detached ailment—we say self, but mean something else. For without others—the Not-self—there would be no self. You remember just now I explained. You recall my argument? No, I am afraid there is nothing for it—your storm of stupid questions has blown the veil off my eyes. I am enlightened.

HANP. I know I am not clever. I am stupid.

ARGHOL. You are worse than clever—you are unclean. You are a sewer-nature—that we stop our noses at—you come rushing up, with your self-important clatter, out of the house-drains of my Automatic.

HANP. Have you a pistol—what is that? Your automatic, Arghol?

ARGHOL. The same thing. Lift up your head! Yes it is marked. I have never noticed those signs before. You are degenerate.

HANP (*violently*). Attend to your own bloody face—keep your personal remarks to yourself.

(*At the reference to personal appearance Hanp becomes at once another person.*)

ARGHOL. Personal! You do not call yourself a person, do you?

HANP. Never mind what I call myself, Milord Sark!

ARGHOL. Well, I have done with you, anyway.—You are the world, brother, with its family objections to me! So go back now to our bustling Mother Nature, and spit in her face—say it's from Arghol! As to this place, I wish to see you here no more, about that my mind is made up.

HANP. Since when was this your place, to order me about? Anybody would think you could sack who you bloody well pleased! I'll see Throg and put that right! You wish to see me here no more! We'll soon see who's the boss, Throg or you!

ARGHOL. Leave here at once! Your services will not be required after today, you may take that from me.

HANP. Listen to you! A month's notice is it?

ARGHOL. No. Go at once. Here is some money, enough to take you out of this and to carry on with. Look for work elsewhere.

(*He throws down three bank-notes upon the table.*)

HANP. Are these my wages?

ARGHOL. Catch the next up-train. Berlin will be better for you. That is a good spot for you. Your mechanical carcass will thrive there, you will see—you can rot in peace there on the asphalt with no life to disturb you, it is dead. Get out as soon as possible. Here is all the money you will get. So make yourself scarce—you are no longer wanted!

(*Amazement stretches the disciple's face back like a bald-lipped mouthpiece dragged tight over the lips. Slowly it contracts—the eyes diminishing, chin more prominent, clenched like a rheumatic fist.—Arghol's voice rings coldly in the hut, a bell beaten by dull words, in a series of calm strokes. The words only—not the tune of the bell at all—have grown harsher. But at last the words beat virulently—Hanp throws up his head, his eyes carbonic and his complexion lead.*

When Arghol has finished, silence falls like a guillotine between them, severing all remaining bonds, of every order. They both stare for a long time into the face of the other, and then Hanp stands up. The disciple speaks with his own voice, which he has not used now for a number of months. It sounds fresh and brisk to him—it is salt and garish, and the mouth feels different too.)

HANP. Is that all?

(*At the sound of Hanp's voice, no longer borrowed, an expression of relief comes into the face of Arghol. The experiment is at an end—he prepares to turn away and leave the door of the hut. The strain of the mock-life at this particular point has been considerable, upon the underworld of energy of the rebellious muscles. His frigid outburst has not been commensurate with it—he turns away intending to escape.*)

HANP. Glib-tongued sod! You've had your say! I've heard you out! Now you'll hear me!

(*Hanp has been crouching beside the table. He springs up out of the ground, a handful of furious movements—he flings himself upon Arghol tooth and nail, with fist and claw.*

Once more the stars have come down.)

ARGHOL (*releasing in the direction of Hanp a formidable kick*). That is not what I told you to do. Stand back or I shall injure you!

HANP. Two can play at that game!

ARGHOL. No, two cannot—I am not playing. Take up your money from that table and be off!

(*Hanp throws himself upon Arghol more fiercely than before, who, seizing him around the body, picks him up and hurls him down upon the ground. The hut is pushed forward a half-dozen feet by some agency beneath, and the roof opens like the lid of a box, to enable the action to take place within.*)

ARGHOL (*to Hanp upon the ground*). Violent fool! A blow is all you can understand. You want to be conversed with on your stupid skin, in black and blue, in a silly ratatat. You have a brain accessible to bastinado, nothing else!

HANP. Do you think you can say all you bloody well like to me? You will find out your mistake!

ARGHOL. You are not happy until you have dragged your betters down to your beast's plane—sensationalist!

HANP. I'll show you who is the beast yet!

ARGHOL. Brave little chipolata! We are quite the little warrior, are we not!

HANP. Jeer away—I've got your number, my lord Loud-Mouth!

ARGHOL. It is your vanity has required this of me. That gives you importance, I suppose, to have been struck—you never feel the equal of a gentleman except when you feel the contact of his shoe-leather.

HANP. You'll find I can kick too, my fine gentleman!

ARGHOL. Yes, yes, my little fire-eater! By throwing him down there I have given him back his self-respect, I do believe!

(*Hanp raises himself upon an elbow, and crouches, but as if in pain.*)

ARGHOL. Emotion-mongering worm!

HANP. Wait till I'm up, I'll give you worm—I will tear out your tongue!

ARGHOL. You wax too fierce—you forget you are nothing here and not persona grata any longer—you are a spare hand who can be easily replaced. I will order Hotshepsot to turn

you out I think. You are not wanted here—your rage will not
alter that. You had better make up your mind to go. Why
make a fuss?

HANP. Before I go I'll see that I mark you for life, mind that!

ARGHOL (*calling*). Hotshepsot!

(*In response there is a faint tempestuous rumble from the
bowels of the earth. It is Hotshepsot cursing in her subterraneous
chamber. Hanp leaps to his feet as Hotshepsot is called to put
him out and attacks Arghol again violently, who closes with
him, enfolding him in a grand impartial embrace, as if to
smother sleepily all this violence in a big cold comprehensive
hug. They struggle together, knocking over chairs, dishes and
glasses, tripping upon the chopping-block.*

*Arghol's antipathy to death, his anti-manhood, words coming
out of caverns of belief—synthesis that is of the Ideal star-
fighter—all of the instruments of thought, combine to weigh
him down. They resist his swift anarchist effort—as, giddy, he
turns to the physical world at last, prepared to accept pro tem.
its cheap solutions.*

*The great beer-coloured heavens, at the fuss, leap in a fête
of green gaiety. Their immense lines bend like whalebones—
spring back with a slight shudder of instantaneous thunder.*

*Above in the beer-red heavens two charging silver clouds—
their two furious shadows—grapple and fight. The bleak misty
hospital of the horizon grows pale with the fluid of anger. In
one black blow the trees of the canal are wiped out. The hut
shrinks or takes on girth, in epileptic expansion—itself hit by
cantankerous trees, or stormed by a next-door house-wall, become the uprushing segment of a wave. Initiated by Hanp, a
a brief spell of sharp fisticuffs intervenes—upon face and head
they strike each other about equally-matched uppercuts and
hooks. Mask stoic with energy (mind cleaned off slick, stripped
for action—body become brain) Arghol peers forth, like an
air-pilot perched in his fighting-coque. Almost with indolence
he rides the whirlwind and directs the storm.—Peach-flushes
upon silk epiderms—the fierce card-play of thundering fists,
flinging down trump after trump—in a thump—gasp, thump—
gasp, thump—gasp—THUMP! Message and mad counter-message,
dropped down anywhere, reaching the brain in a rattle of morse,
in body telegraphy—the most shattering messages possible.*

The attacker rushes in now boozed with blows and winded with a big smack under the left tit. They roll, swift jagged rut, into a corner of the hut—a headlong insect, of tropical proportions, at the sound of footsteps scuttling to cover. Both stop astonished pulled up by the wall. Fisticuffs again: then they roll kicking off at a fierce tangent.

But the punch of Hanp rapidly wears itself out upon these herculean clouds—the insect-rut is slowed down—a lethargy bemuses the attacker. Then like a punch-ball, something vague, swift and mechanical strikes Hanp in the face, as it is stuck up white and exhausted after a volley. It is Arghol hitting. He strikes out impartially at nothing in particular.

The hitting is not very hard—only occurring as rebound, and as attacked—the larger machine behaving like an impersonal thing, but equipped for a mechanical tit-for-tat. Arghol has become the soft, blunt paw of Nature—taken back to her bosom, as a matter of course—slowly and idly winning her battle!

The Enemy of the Stars has of a sudden become solidary with the massive landscape. Its springs have become his springs, it is he who is at the heart now of its occult resistances. The key to the commotion, the frantic fist of Hanp, drums and taps more erratically upon this elastic mass he has attacked. Then the entire sky seems to inflict upon him a gentle unexpected electrical back-hander—a lightning-touch, and all is put out at once. He falls flat somewhere in the shadow, there he lies. Time itself effects the count of nine, and the knock-out is established—Hanp has been put to sleep.—Convective fists at droop, the battle over, the new Champion of the Universe *stands rigid, staring out into the yard as if listening for something, his brows furrowed and nostrils dilated. But the nervous geometry of the world-in-sight relaxes. It goes on with its perpetual mystic invention. Arghol throws himself down where before he has been lying.*

A strong flood of suppressed thinking passes up to the fatigued head of the muscular saint, and it dazes him. His mind was out of training. It is puffed and exhilarated, ideas and sensations fall upon it like punches upon a body out of trim. His mind, that iron-throated mastiff with the big blank bay, he flings off as it sets up its death-howl. In a steep struggle, to this insistent mental music, he rolls heavily into sleep. Now a dark dream begins valuing, with its tentative symbols, the foregoing events.)

ARGHOL DREAMS.

A black jacket and shirt are suspended upon picture-nails across the window. The gas-jet is turned down at half-cock, to supply some heat to the room through the chill and sallow brilliance of the northern night. There are two pillows, unequally fletched, stained and depressed in their brown centres by the weight of an unwashed head of large size, but congested at either extremity. Bed-clothes crawl over the bed that is never made, like an embossed crust of stagnant waves, to be crept beneath but not disturbed. Above the pillow a Rosabonheurish litho of plump cart-horses (trampling up the wall like well-fed toffyish insects). Books piled upon table and chairs, open at some page in nine cases out of ten—six open books in pickaback ascent, in elevation to the dust-choked plane of a stout pine mantelshelf.

Two texts in Finnish admonish the pillowed summit of the bed. Pipes, half-smoked, collars and cuffs of indiarubber. The days of the preceding week are not effaced beneath the besom and the duster, but souvenirs of their accidents remain jettisoned in scraps and middens.

His room in the city—nine feet by twelve—grave big enough for the six corpses that is each living person!

But at the sight of this student-chamber he falls into a passion: he tears down the jacket and the shirt, and throws open the window. As he does so he starts back. At the fresh air of the morning of his life striking him in the face he is overcome with giddiness. He begins to put things straight, however. The third book, stalely open at a neglected passage, its surface stained with dust, which he takes up to shut, is 'Einzige und Sein Eigentum.'

Stirner. Well! That bad offshoot of the master of Marx in his prime! That constipated philosopher of action.

One of the seven arrows in his martyr mind!

Poof! he flings it out of the open window—it takes wing with all its pages spread. A rapid minute, and a quiet knock comes at the door. A young man known to him in the university town, but now seen for the first time, walks briskly in. 'Good morning!' He has come up to bring back the book. The book has plunged into the roadway—laughs from the visitor as he informs him of its unexpected descent, among some persons following a hearse, who took it as an omen! Very good, indeed! Very, ha ha!

'I thought I told you to get out?' Arghol exclaims.

The undergraduate has changed into his present follower.

Obliquely—though he appears now to be addressing Stirner
—he shouts out—'I thought I told you we should need your
services no more!'

A third time his visitor has changed. Now he sees before him
a middle-aged man, red-cropped head, and dark proud purple
eyes—evidently a philosopher! Self-possessed, loose, free,
student-sailor-fashion, fingering the discarded book: coming to
a decision.—Stirner, in fact, as he had first imagined him.

'Leave here at once! It is absurd. You have ceased to be persona grata. Here are three notes—nine dollars. Go at once!'

*   *   *   *

Was the money for the book, or what? Of what were these
dollar-bills in settlement? Were they too much? It seemed so.

The man flings the book suddenly at his head, its cover slaps
him sharply on the cheek—what next?

'Glib-tongued defaulter—take that! Never trick! Honesty's
the best policy!'

A scrap ensues. Physical experiences of recent fight recur,
ending in violent expulsion of the ill-smelling visitor. There is
the sharp slamming of the door.

'These books are all parasites,' Arghol exclaims. 'Poodles of
the mind I call them—just Chows and Charleses. Eternal prostitute—"I shall always be!"—If you understand what I mean by
that!'

A great boisterous talking is set up now in his wandering
consciousness.

'The mind, perverse and gorgeous. All the world of book-
worms, and the verbal poodles, should be discouraged to my
way of thinking. All this Art-life—posterity and the rest of it is
rank nonsense—it should be struck at! Start with these!'

He tears up his books. There are several hundred. A pile by
the door is ready to sweep out. He leaves the room, and makes
for the nearby Café to find his friends, the other students. As
he goes he mutters:

'All companions of the parasite Self—not one of them is a
brother, in fact far from it—my traffic with these fellows is
with their parasites. I am the Self.'

Head down, he hastens forward, to surprise these parasites. The night suddenly has come on. Stars like a clear rain soak into him with a delicious chill in the marrow. Nobody is in the street—it is a perfectly deserted city, of the dead in fact. The sickly houses ooze a sad human electricity. It had been his sudden intention to spring-clean spiritually—to fumigate his quarters. Accumulations of Self must be treated as deliberate refuse—a similar purging now must be undertaken among his companions. This is preparatory, of course, to his leaving the city for ever and a day. Heigh-ho!

But he never reaches the Weinstube. The dream changes. He is walking down the main street of his native town—his present address. He knows no one but his school-mates—there are workmen, clerks in import and export of hemp, grain, timber and alcohol, he just knows and salutes. But ahead of him, not many feet, one of his student friends from the state-capital walks forward looking to left and right. He neglects to ask himself how the fellow has got there, but he catches him up and strikes him on the shoulder. Although brusquely pitched elsewhere in this fashion, Arghol perseveres with his late plan.

'Sir, I wish to know you!'

A provisional smile forces its way into the face of the puzzled acquaintance, who stands still; he has held him up, firing off his question.

'Ah, Arghol. You seem upset. Is this where you live?'

'Of course. I desire to make your acquaintance, sir. Do you object? I have no card with me. May I present myself?'

'But, my dear fellow, what can be the matter with you? We are already very well acquainted. Don't you remember me?'

'I am not Arghol.'

'No? You must excuse me for doubting you, when you say that! You were Arghol when last I saw you.'

Such smug security, on the part of this well-balanced person, offends the fanatical Arghol greatly, as is only natural—he frowns, he clears his throat. Such a superficial fellow as this would never see anyone but the customary Arghol of his acquaintance—the first one to whom he had been introduced, with a click of heels, in the hall of a Mensur. Did not these clear-cut identifications, of Mister this and Mister that, give to this easy-going person the system of definitions which constitutes a person 'normal'? That was so. Arghol—that creature of two-dimensions, clumsily cut out in cardboard by the coarse scissor-work of the short-sighted group-spirit—the social mind —that impudent parasite had forgathered too long with men, borne his name too variously, to be easily abashed much less ousted. Why, he was not sure, even had they been separated surgically, in which self life would have gone out, and in which kept alight.

'This man has been masquerading as me!' is what he wished to remark. He would repudiate Arghol. If the eyes of his friends-up-till-then could not be opened, he would sweep the entire assemblage of them from childhood up, playmates and patrons, along with the preposterous Arghol, into the dust heap. The fellow Arghol was under a dishonouring pact with the group—this he spits on and tears up.

'So I am Arghol. This is who you think I am, sir?'

'Of course. But if you don't want to be Arghol, we will say no more about it!'

'That is a lie. Your foolish grin proves you are lying. Good day to you, sir—and I hope you will see your way to leave this town before another night has passed. Adieu!'

Walking on with a quick rolling stride, he knows this fellow to be in fact his Arghol-self from the aftertaste of his voice. He has divested himself of something—that is good. The second pair of footsteps follow, however—an odious invitation is contained in the polite timing of these indelicate softly-falling steps. But gradually the sound of the never-quite-merging footfalls of the Shadow-being send him to sleep. Fallen in this way into a second slumber, again he dreams—it is 'fate' that he should always be sleeping. Next, a Weinstube. He is writing. At the other end of the apartment his friends are seated, they have him under observation. It is exactly as it had in fact come to pass—before he returned to take up work in the home-business there had been this situation in the cafés. There he is at all events, behaving as though he were a perfect stranger with a whole set of persons with whom he had been on terms of intimacy the day before.

'He's a case for the clinic.' They were tapping their temples. 'Poor old Arghol! Leave him alone,' they advise each other. 'This has been coming on for some time now.'

Abruptly, through a confused succession of struggles and a multitude of scenes, a new consciousness asserts itself—once more he becomes Arghol, with a big blush of bursting self-awareness. Could this be a key to something? If so, he should lay hold of it!

'I am Arghol!' he finds himself exclaiming with satisfaction, as pleased as Punch to be plain Arghol again, and no nonsense.

He repeats the name loudly to himself—like a sinister trade-name coined for the launching of a brand-new toilet article, to storm the town in super-capitals—toilet-necessity, he, to scrub the psyche of all lesser men, a public lavabo.—He had ventured into his solitude and failed there—but Arghol he had supposed left behind in the city is suddenly here, who has followed him, almost a stowaway. And lo, it is Hanp! Which at least clears up an ambiguity—always à deux—the old Arghol has been born again! The prodigal has returned—he is back at the starting-post.

(Hanp lies bleeding—for some time he is on his back recovering in a dull convulsion. Then his brain commences to function. Chattel for rest of mankind—it tells him with a hiss—he has been brutalized by this chattel! Things even, or men like things, rise up and trample on him! Both his eyes are a blue and bursting pulp. So shut in, so cut off from the visible world, reflexion is doubly difficult. But a great sullen indignation lowers in him against Arghol, for passing over into Action after all he has said—he who had not the right to act at all.

In him was not Action in fact indecent? Here was a question of taste: the heavy body, so long quiet, flinging itself destructively about—face strained with the intimate expression of the act of love—what a repulsive picture was that, as it shot up in retrospect, reel after reel. The massive grip of the false saint's biceps still impressed itself upon his person, in outrageous squeezes.

'In races accustomed to restraint, is not pudeur the most violent emotion?' that great extraordinary talking man had recently thrown out as a leading question. 'The Devil Ridicule, and the God of Taste,' said he, 'between them, control the powerfullest springs of action. Why have not the operations of these fatal divinities been adopted as a basis of Northern Tragedy—as the basis I should be inclined to put it at that.'

So the operations of these fatal divinities had been compelled by their discoverer to produce their tragedy at last. The Northern Drama in excelsis, better than Niebelungen or Volsungen, had been duly staged, its image struck—its values minted and put in circulation. Here was the seed of an epical Hamlet. Here was the novel formula, for the most ancient impulses in the Northern consciousness. The violent rape of the ascetic mind! Hanp had played Tarquin to this embattled purity. He had come opposing the vigorous animal glorification of self to the fierce humility of the perverse ascetic. The latter he had ravished with his indecent violence, in the very sanctuary of the anchorite.

Hanp considers, unable to rise from the corner of the cabin, what his next step must be. To go home is the best course under the circumstances, to live there for a while upon his good-natured drunken mother, recriminating and savage at night but good for a little money in the morning, for her favourite chick as he was, and so take things easy. But in the spectacle of that tipsy domesticity stretching back to babyhood Hanp detects a family likeness to the present events. He recalls how, seeing that she was weak and easy-going when sober, he had considered the same woman had no right to be violent and resentful when tight. Now, scrutinizing the past, he recognizes in her handsome sodden features an odd look of Arghol. He spits. The taint of this old hen is in him, his flesh and blood! But these are familiar sensations insinuated into his imagination by the great extraordinary talking-fellow at whose hands he has just received a regulation knock-out—he has been made to turn and spit upon his own flesh and blood in disgust, by this great magical talking creature who has been thrashing him in self-defence or has lured him on to get a beating.

The glutted mass of the victor, as if he had made a square meal off the weaker vessel and inferior pugilist, shows a dark heaving outline against the brilliant yard. Is that a hoarded energy, acquired from others—has that passivity of his ever been holy, with the charm of the saint? Or has it been a sham quietness? Of course the great rolled-up rotter was sleepy now —he had had his fill of action for a bit again! Even the great curled-up brute's physical strength was obnoxious—no flabby fat could be more so! Ah these chains of perfect muscles! They made you vomit at their steel.

Lying there by the door, he heaves. It is in a sickly pneumatic pumping of stale wind. Death the refrain of his being, Arghol lies now, like a corpse (fitted with a wheezing pump). But the great humbug's preparation for extinction, in which all

*his days are passed, is a ritual to scare it off if anything, rather
than a going-out to meet it! Why not tip him over into the
cauldron into which he persistently gazes? It is an irresistible
notion—as a mere sleepy desire, to commence with, it visits
the brooding battered senses, with the convalescent disciple,
at the tail of a hundred other restless images. It comes in at
the end after the manner of a circus clown, vaulting upon a
horse's caparisoned back, when the family of elegant riders
have hopped, with obsequious dignity, down the gangway that
conducts to the wings—not to be taken seriously.*

*Bluebottle, at first unremarked, hurtling stealthily—a stout
snore rises into the air. Clotted, soulless and self-centred, it
compels hysteria—flooding up into his congested neck, as
Hanp listens. The first organ-note abates—but a second ponder-
ously is set up—stronger and more startling than the first. It
purrs a little now, rapid and labial. Then it is virile and strident
again, stentorian and long-drawn-out—it rises and falls up the
centre of the listener's body, a peachy, clotted tide of sound,
gurgling back into the viscous shallows. It is the snorting of a
malodorous, bloody sink, emptying its water. Now it speaks to
him—it is a trumpet-call not to battle but to murder—it plunges
into his mind with bestial regularity, in and out again, purblind
and self-confident. Hanp lies in a dull sweat, stopping his ears, his
face pressed against the ground. At each fresh offence the veins
puff faintly in his temples. All the majestic sonority of this voice
that in the past sometimes has subdued him, suddenly turned
into music of the disrespectful Abyss, anti-human rhapsodies of
the waste-pipe and water-closet, to order—it was more than he
could stand up to, this was the authentic coup de grâce.)*

HANP. If you don't stop I'll wring your bloody neck! I'll
slit your slimy gizzard as soon as look at you—stop that!

(*A head rises above the floor-level at the rear of the
hut, out of the trap descending into the players' quarters.
It is Hotshepsot. She remains a head only, of an observer
dropped up to watch for a spell, she does not come up
any more out of the trap.*)

HOTSHEPSOT. The devil is asleep!

HANP (*groaning and turning stiffly in her direction*). Yes,
he's taking forty winks. How do you like the music?

HOTSHEPSOT. Beautiful! Does he treat you to that every
night?

HANP. No. This is an exception.

HOTSHEPSOT. What was all that noise I heard? (*Looking round the hut, at the disorder*) Have you been taking it out of him?

HANP. No, he's been taking it out of me!

HOTSHEPSOT. What *that*! You surprise me. You must be a mild-mannered man and no mistake to let him come any rough stuff with you! You must be a good deal meeker than I thought!

HANP. Perhaps. He's twice my size. He's as strong as an ox, as a matter of fact.

HOTSHEPSOT. Well, well. This is something quite new. I'm sorry the big boy hurt you. I thought you could look after yourself!

HANP. Perhaps.

HOTSHEPSOT. That great gas-bag there wouldn't say boo to a goose. He must have been surprised to find someone to knock about for a change!

HANP. Perhaps. But what do you want anyway, bum-face?

HOTSHEPSOT. Not you, whatever else not that—I should want a better man than you, especially now you're marked like that!

HANP. You'd be lucky to find one at all, with such a wart in place of a dial! Soft pears don't grow on every bush.

HOTSHEPSOT. I'll leave you to enjoy the concert.

HANP. You won't be missed.

HOTSHEPSOT. You're a pretty pair. He's poached your eyes for you properly! Well, so long—call me if you want any help!

(*Hanp throws a lump of turf at the head and it disappears, with a grimace of contumelious scorn and a parting snort from lips of red disdain.*)

KING SNORE

In a long whinnying rasp, Hanp's spirit is drawn out of him, a few more blasts and he will be a yelling wreck as flabby as a degassed air-ball. Battened upon by this brazen sound, he looks round him wildly. But the rigor of his exquisite discomfort changes. It is a sly volte-face, of Nature's art. Glee settles thickly down—he listens to the tall notes of the filthy trumpet with a deep hysterical relish. The snore crows out with a gathering loudness. It is glad seemingly in sympathy with him.

The old Snore laughs almost as it mounts the murky scale, for very cheerfulness, to think that at last the arch-listener should have learnt to appreciate it—better late than never and all that sort of thing.—A rare and proper world, if only you know how to take it—and so forth! So the Snore snortles and Hanp hastens to agree.

He gets upon his feet in a stealthy uprightness, encompassed by this foul sound of sleep. His vitals are wrung by the bold falsetto of its extreme vibrations. But his lips smile the smile of the beatific mystic. The world shall be ridded of this outrageous instrumentalist. His, Hanp's, shall be the hand of God. Peeping in a dim puppy-stare, through tumefied slits of blackened flesh, he sways and groans a little. A booze-hound collecting his wits, he fumbles in his hip-pocket, then in his thigh-pocket, then in his chest-pocket. His knife is absent, he removes his hand. For the duration of a Snore, he stands, wiping the blood off his neck and chin, then moves across the hut to where the circular mass of Arghol commences, with the outline of his booted feet. The Snore blares out again, to greet him. Its recoveries possess an alarming quality, as if of the powerful love-call of a substantial snouted quadruped (of the stoat sort). Each time it trumpets afresh, he hangs back and gasps—suppressing a clap of girlish laughter which effervesces in his throat.

Meanwhile he peers about carefully, on all hands, next—with his eyes as if provided with portentous dust-goggles from the boxing-match. He remarks the chopper, which has flown out of the hand of Hotshepsot, when he tumbled her into the companion-hatch. As he sights this property he starts forward. An ocean of movements pours into his body—he stretches and strains like a big toy in the act of being wound-up. He draws in a series of deep breaths—his eyes in their puffed clefts almost invisible—one of them he opens up roughly with two fingers, the chopper held stiffly at arm's-length. Now he can see Arghol plainly—the big slumbering death-mask, the stretched-out throat—its tempting arteries. He kneels down beside the sleeper —a prolonged snore drives his hand back, which has approached that it may rehearse the blow. But his arm goes quickly a long distance back and stands up stiffly in the air, the gleaming cleaver kissed by the starlight. Sighting upon the blond-skinned throat, with a furious swing he brings it rushing down, and it chops heavily into the glistening column of meat. The blood bursts out after the blade as it breaks in. Again he raises it into the air and swiftly strikes, to sever the whole head if possible—if he can get in one more double-handed chop with his hand-guillotine, that might be easy, and the face fly from the trunk!

At the first of the blows Arghol has clutched the ground and a fat snore expires in a sudden blood-bath, with an angry gurgle. At the second, half-decapitated he suddenly rises, as though propelled by a spring, his eyes glaring across at Hanp and with a convulsive action of the head as though he were about to sneeze. Hanp shrinks back upon his haunches at this resurrection.

ARGHOL (*his hand at his throat, blood issuing from his mouth as he opens it*). Ah, tiger, you have kept your birth-tryst—you are here with your sharp axe!

HANP (*moving away, muttering*). It was your doing.

ARGHOL. You have killed me—and to excuse yourself—say it is I who have done it—how like you that last action is!

HANP. It was you! I have done nothing.

ARGHOL. Because I could not speak your tongue—in your barbarity!

HANP. You forced me, liar! All along, what were you doing?

ARGHOL. A question of words.

HANP. Words? Deeds! These are not words!

ARGHOL. Tell Nature—she was behind your arm—tell Nature—the job is done!

Arghol rises a foot into the air, his arm outstretched, his red hand flourished in the other's face. Hanp overbalances and falls upon his back.

Scrambling up swiftly, with a loud bleat of fear, Hanp discovers the other in the position in which he had been sleeping more or less, he has rolled back into an untidy coil. His head is thrust out into the yard. Hanp gazes down, not at all sure of it —all flesh is the same and this is flesh: but he fixes his dilated eye upon it, in the expectation that it may refuse to suffer such a straightforward 'fate' at all.

Something distant, terrible, and eccentric, bathing in that sickly snore, has been struck down and forever banished from Matter. That he at last comes to recognize, and slowly he moves away. He wipes his hands upon a rag, looks towards the dark mouth of the shaft at the back of the roofless apartment, and then passes out of the hut into the yard. Suddenly all about him the electric night has grown particularly peaceful—attempting richly to please this official trespasser, the servant of the stars, with the gracious movements of its trees, or gay processions of glittering arctic cloudbanks. Immense relief throughout of the starry universe—congratulating itself heartily upon the news of this political assassination of first-class importance. He is the darling of the sky for a few minutes, when he first steps out. But a galloping blackness of mood overtakes the lonely figure. Quickly he moves forward to outstrip it perhaps. Near the ornamental crested gateway of the ancient figure-yard Hanp encounters a lounging idle shadow. It is Sfox. He grinds his teeth almost in this faceless helm, of a mask of inexpressive clay, with a movement of furious aggression in its direction. The blank face looks shy and pleased, but civil, participating in the general sentiments of all things at that moment—all except Hanp, that is true.

Very slowly the solitary figure of Hanp (observed by the faceless super Sfox) approaches the stone bridge over the canal, not far from the opal cloudlet. His face is wet with tears, his heart stamps weakly up and down within his chest, a sickly flood of moonlight beats miserably down upon him from across the water, cutting out an empty shadow behind him, which with difficulty he can summon the strength to drag forward. With a clumsy recklessness, like a bad actor—or else one in violent disagreement with his part, or fed up with the company and out to disgrace them with his casualness—Hanp springs off the parapet of the bridge. It is the poorest suicide that was ever staged, he might have been jumping into a swimming bath in a fit of ill-temper. He sinks like the plummet in the imagery of his murdered master, heavy with hatred and nothing left to work it off on—so quite certain to go to the bottom and stop there. A big conspicuous splash of silver spray, and the second figure in the cast disappears abruptly from view. EXIT SECOND PLAYER WITHIN THE WATERS OF THE CANAL, in other words.

A black cloud enters and occupies the whole arena, immediately everything is blotted out. Accompanying the cloud a wind is heard sighing high up in the vertical tunnel. Then there is no sound in particular and only the blackness of a moonless and unstarlit night.

PHYSICS OF THE
NOT-SELF

This essay is in the nature of a metaphysical commentary upon the ideas suggested by the action of *Enemy of the Stars*. Briefly, it is intended to show the human mind in its traditional rôle of the enemy of life, as an oddity outside the machine. In the first of the ensuing sections, for instance, that entitled 'Catonic Truth,' it is shown how the egotistic falsehood of Cato is more generally acceptable than the scrupulousness of the philosopher. Of all things in the world liable to arouse men's apprehension, it is clear that 'the scientific truth about anything' has a good claim to the first place. In it they scent, with reason, the principle of death. They do not scent this in natural science, because science has disguised itself more effectually as 'a thing,' or as 'nature.' No one, to illustrate this, is afraid of being bitten by a motor-car—though he, of course, might go mad if bitten by a scientist. And he has, of course, recently (1914-18) been slaughtered in very great numbers by what living men undeniably had invented.

Disguised as 'nature,' and taking on the impersonality and 'inscrutableness' of natural laws, a small but picked number of men have put themselves at the head of the forces of nature, as it were, in their old struggle with Man. The results so far have been startling enough. But it is hoped, shortly, that nature will, with their assistance, achieve a really decisive and annihilating success—with regard to the human race a really *smashing* victory!

The guns, bombs and gas in the Great War did not enlighten people. This was because it was supposed to be merely cruel Mother Nature eating up her children—obliged to do so, of course, in consequence of the Darwinian law that exacts such destruction. When you are dealing with 'a law'—then there is nothing further to be said! Then, the penalty of lifts, telephones and crystal sets must fatally, and as a matter of course, be commensurate with their advantages. High buildings 'grow' —do they not? And the fatigue of climbing them is neutralized by the escalator. For this advantage life and limb are mortgaged —as we should expect, should we not?

Without pursuing the subject further, it will be understood from this brief note what order of things is in question in the pages that follow.

CATONIC TRUTH

'I would not believe it even if Cato told me,' was a Roman saying. But the *truthfulness* of Cato would be the last refinement, of course, of the effrontery of the oligarch. The 'we truthful ones' of Nietzsche is the lyrical equivalent—perjury being the characteristic humiliation imposed by his circumstances upon the serf. To judge from the accounts of his contemporaries, Cato must have been as terrible a man as it would be easy to find: and Cato's 'truth' would be what Cato thought, and his legendary exactitude would include, no doubt, every variety of brassy outspokenness. For Cato was not a man to go out of his way to *look for* truth; he would take 'truth' as he found it, as, in short, it welled up from the source of his egotism. He would no doubt suppress anything presenting itself to his mind and claiming to be 'truth' which had not the authentic hallmark of catonic directness—which was not *wished*, or was not wanted. And, like that 'liberty' which might not survive the death of Cato, so 'truth', it is a fair assumption, would not survive him either, or anything else 'that was his'—so relative must Cato's 'truth' have been.

The philosopher, who is more uncertain about truth, is therefore proverbially unsatisfactory in the catonic sense. His scruples brand him as a liar from the start—since he is apt to stammer, if not blush, when first asked a question. Even when, after a painful effort, he reaches an affirmation, it is so beset with reservations that it remains a particularly offensive sort of lie for those who prefer the will's truth to that of the intellect. The *not-self* established in the centre of the intellect betrays at every moment its transient human associate. The wise man, in consequence (the opposite of that pitiful object, the philosopher), keeps it locked up, a skeleton in a cupboard, or an abnormal offspring that it would be disastrous to exhibit. And if anyone refers to the existence of that unfortunate byproduct of the human state, they convict themselves on the spot of being *no gentleman*, or, at the best, an enemy. Thus to doubt a man's word, a wise man's, can surely be regarded as an oblique reference to this intellectual abortion or death's-head under lock and key.

THE MAN OF HIS WORD

What results from these observations may be formulated as follows. There is a thing popularly referred to as 'truth' somewhere or other—never mind where. Of this fact all men born of women are aware. Just as, by analogy with ourselves, and in response to the dictates of the physiologic norm, we know that every creature of flesh and blood consummates the digestive sequence in a certain manner, so we know that he likewise harbours this attribute—of 'truth.' The same rules apply to this disgraceful instrument of the intellect as govern the final stages of that act, the first stage of which is ingestion (which first stage it is recognized shall be permitted to occur in public).

If you ask two men, or if two men came to be asked in a court of law, what happened upon a certain day some months earlier, you can tell almost at once which is the *truthfuller* of the two. Probably one, without hesitation—frankly and freely—will give his answer. But the other will be confused, and will display every sign of a most guilty uncertainty. *The former* man is the man you respect—whose 'word,' you know, is worthy of credence, and probably 'as good as his bond.' He is the 'man of his word.' His word is *his own* word. The other man's 'word' might be anybody's!

The latter man, you would say, is a 'man of words.' But the former securely possesses, as a lightly-held property, the tame word, which obediently represents the man and his interests. The latter (the 'man of words') is a slave, the former (the 'man of his word') is a free-man. The latter is afraid of a 'word': the former is not afraid of any 'word.' One will sacrifice himself to a mere 'word,' the other would see any 'word' hanged first. The latter is the man you will instinctively *trust*.

THE ENEMY OF THE STARS

If 'truth' is the word we give to that disintegrated *not-self* principle which every man necessarily must harbour (but which he can be trained quite easily to paralyse), then every altruism can be traced to the activities of this same principle. But from this it must not be supposed that the destruction of this principle in a man cuts him off from 'his fellows.' That would be a great mistake. The contrary is, in fact, the case.

The man who has formed the habit of consulting and adhering to the principle of the *not-self* participates, it is true, in

the life of others outside himself far more than does the contrary type of man, he who *refrains* from making any use at all
of this speculative organ. But he is not, for that reason, *more
like* other people. He is *less like* them. For is he not one in a
great many thousand? And to be like other people he certainly should be less them and more himself. Hence his altruism
only results in differentiating him, and in leaving him without
as it were a 'class,' even without a 'kind.' For this ultra-human
activity is really inhuman: even it frustrates its own purpose
by awakening suspicion instead of trust. It is regarded as a
breaker-down of walls, a dissolvent of nations, factions, and
protective freemasonries, a radio-active something in the
midst of more conservative aggregations, as naturally it is. It is
an enemy principle. It is heartily disliked. Since, again, by its
very nature, it awakens love, that is not in its favour either.
Love being the thing that is most prized by men, the individual
who (in league with the diabolical principle of the *not-self*)
appears to be attempting to obtain it by unlawful means is at
once without the pale. By way of the intellect he is necessarily
reaching what the force and fraud of brute nature are otherwise combined to obtain (and of which they get very little).

The intellect, or the seat of that forbidden principle of the
not-self, is the one thing that every gentleman is sworn, however hard pressed, never to employ. What cannot be obtained
by way of self—by that great public road of private fraud—
must be foregone. That is understood, universally recognized
(by all White Men and pukka 'sports'). The intellect is the
devil, it could be said. But more than that, there is something
indefinably *disreputable* about it. It is not 'clean.' It cannot be
described confidently as 'white.' It is not 'the thing.' It is un-
questionably not 'top drawer.' It is irreparably un-pukka. It is,
in the last analysis, the enemy of all the constellations and
universes.

We have *one* life, and we have *one* individuality. It is a ration,
as it were. It is an 'obligation' (so people say sometimes about
'art') to devote all our energies to that one self, and not to
poach. We were not born twenty men, but one. It is our duty 'to
remain in our class.' Equally it is our duty to remain in our self
—our one and only. But if we *must* go out of our 'class,' then
it is 'a sacred duty' to get into a higher one at least. And if we
must go outside our self—if we are so wrong-headed—then at

least it is our 'bounden duty' to see that we do not, at least, despoil ourselves for others. We must go outside in order to *take*, not in order to *give*. But it is far more dignified to remain closeted with one's inalienable physical possessions—like a sedate hen upon its eggs—from the cradle to the grave. Oh, yes: that certainly is so.

THE HUSBANDRY OF 'GOODNESS'

If it is true that any lie becomes the 'truth' when one *wants* it to be that—that, by merely *wishing*, a really determined man can 'make anything of anything,' and transform black (in the chemistry of his desire) into the most dazzling white—following the catonic, the roman, method: then it is also and by the same token true that altruism, or generosity, can be so rigidly related to his interests that never a drop is wasted: and that, in fact with usury, its store is seen constantly to augment.

All other sorts of 'givers' are, not unjustifiably, mistrusted. A gift that *expects no return* is not a human gift. No man has a right to bestow in that way. The chances that he is a god or an angel are so very slender that some peculiarly despicable form of theft is evidently contemplated. It will require all the victim's energy to frustrate this criminal intention. No 'goodness' succeeds like successful 'goodness,' in other words. If you are respectable, then you can only accept things from a person who evidently benefits more than you do as a consequence of his bounty.

It will be profitable for this argument at present to examine briefly the old status of 'goodness,' and to see what it has become in our time—after a prolonged association in the popular mind with sexual morality, especially.

GREEK 'GOODNESS'

At the end of the *Symposium*, Socrates is described as persuading the last of the revellers that 'the same person is able to compose both tragedy and comedy, and that the foundations of the tragic and the comic arts are essentially the same.'

Since there is a unique point of common emotion from which these two activities arise, to which both can be traced back (and on account of which common source the same poet is enabled to excel at both), so no doubt the different categories of forms, and their archetypes, would be fused, for such a mind, somewhere or other, into one composite body. No doubt beauty, pity, justice and the rest of the socratic predicates would melt into each other in some more general perfection. But *arete*, which we translate goodness, seems less specialized than most of them: and 'goodness' in its modern sense is, as a translation, misleading.

John Burnet tells us that 'goodness,' for a Greek, had no ethical significance. 'We are left in no doubt as to what "goodness" (*arete*) meant in the language of the time . . . it was, in fact, what we call efficiency. To the Greeks goodness was always something positive': and so on. Liddell and Scott have for *arete* 'goodness, excellence of any kind, especially of manly qualities, valour, etc.' Also 'excellence in any art.' They cite Plato as the authority for its ethical use. But Burnet, as we see above, does not agree to this. Like 'virtue' in English, it may have traversed several meanings—the utilitarian, the martial, and something like the christian. *Excellence* in anything is, however, what Burnet sticks to. And Burnet is a great authority: he even says it meant for the sophists 'little more than skill in the arts of party intrigue.'

But Socrates has several 'goodnesses': his highest philosophical goodness (*philosophike arete*), is the one identified with knowledge, and which can be taught, like a trade: and there is a popular 'goodness' of the lower order.

In the *Phaedo* (81-82), Socrates shows what happens at the close of this life to the bad man; and whatever *arete* may have meant to a fifth-century Athenian, it is quite evident what is meant by it in this socratic dialogue. The soul of the philosopher goes to dwell with 'that which resembles it, the invisible divine, immortal and wise'; in a place 'excellent, pure and invisible.' The unjust, and the only popularly 'good,' are, in Socrates' ethical Zoo, allotted their respective shapes. Asses, wolves, hawks and kites are inhabited by souls that have shown their aptitude for such destinies as these lives imply. The 'good' citizen, however, may hope to become a bee, a wasp or an ant. For, like all the ancients, Socrates idealized these small industrious machines.

This goodness which is essentially an excellence, like excellence in craft, and which merges into the wisdom and piety of the philosopher, is like the upanishadic Karma; and the returns to the animal world, or the annihilation and peace in the bosom of the Absolute, or Brahman, are similarly parallel to the Indian conception.

The 'knowledge' that is identified with 'goodness' is, like goodness, of two kinds in Plato: the less empirical knowledge being called *doxa* (belief) and only the Eternal lending itself to such knowledge as can deserve the name of *episteme*. This epistemological absolute is much the same as Brahman; and the inferior knowledge of the world of temporal experience is much the same as the upanishadic *avidya*. The quality of the known and the object of knowledge, and the impossibility of anything but a wisdom of metaphors, glimpses and trances, in terrestrial life, you get in Socrates and in Plato as with the Indian (*cf.* the subject of Yâ jñaval Kya: 'Thou canst not see the seer of seeing, thou canst not hear the hearer of hearing, thou canst not comprehend the comprehender of comprehending, thou canst not know the knower of knowing').

Socrates (in the ecstatic language of physical life, it is true) taught abstention from bodily desire. Philosophy gives freedom from the obscenities of existence. 'Imprisoned' in the body, using it and its senses only *just as much as is necessary* (otherwise 'the soul reels like an intoxicated man,' inflamed and disordered by contact with the objects of sense), you should abstract yourself, and, as far as possible, withdraw your mind till it passes momentarily into the cathartic peace of the Eternal. 'Philosophy . . . endeavours to free the soul by showing that the view of things by means of the eyes is full of depression, as also is that through the ears and the other senses, persuading an abandonment of these so far as it is not absolutely necessary to use them, and to believe nothing else he hears . . . for that a thing of this kind (one which differs under different aspects) is sensible and visible, but what she herself perceives is intelligible and invisible' (*Phaedo* 83).

This is an invitation to plunge into the 'soul,' the opposite of the plunge into Life suggested by Bergson. Instead of outside, inside. It is an invitation that has often been repeated. Perhaps 'the soul' is sometimes *at home* and sometimes *not*. There may be some ages when you are likely to find it rushing about outside: others when the inside-plunge is the likeliest to be rewarded with success. People as far as their own egos are concerned possess an instinct where this erratic psyche is; and, in fact, in most ages, the great majority have plunged *outwards*.

The empirical world, the *eidola* of Plato, then, could yield nothing but a spurious knowledge. And the conception of knowledge as the highest goal—identified with goodness—was the same as the supreme upanishadic conception. To *know* the atman, to *know* yourself, appeared the supreme efficiency in both systems. The fusion of the idea of goodness with that of knowledge we see in the teaching of Mani, for that matter; with his Persian ontology, the principles of Dark and Light, he taught that as the mind of a person contains increasingly more light, so it contains correspondingly more goodness. Socrates held that it was impossible for a man to *understand* and to be evil. This is usually regarded as the supreme example of socratic unwisdom: the most 'irritating' of all his many challenges to common sense. 'The question involved in the argument with Polemarchus is really the same. Is it possible to regard goodness as a purely neutral accomplishment of this kind, or is it something that belongs to the very nature of this soul that possesses it so that it is really impossible for the good man to do evil or to injure anyone?' (J. Burnet).

If it is in the introduction of ethical and æsthetic forms upon a footing of equality with the mathematical that the originality of Socrates, as the successor of the Pythagoreans, reposes, then in a sense ethics is only introduced to be disposed of; for the *skill-cum-knowledge-goodness* of Socrates, or the approximation to perfect knowledge, are very mathematical conceptions, when compared with those of more emotional ethics. The idea, in its simplest development, seems to amount to this:

1. It is the philosopher's business to dispose of all desire.
2. If you know or understand *fully* you no longer desire.
3. It is the philosopher's business to *know* as fully as possible.
4. In this way the socratic 'goodness' is seen to be the same as Nirvana.
5. And with regard to this statement: You can only be just, moderate and beneficent if you are not involved in what you are called to act upon—if you are withdrawn from it and 'not interested in it.'
6. Therefore the ruler should be a philosopher—in order that he may dispose of what he rules over, as though he were an indifferent god.

There is, in short, no emotional value attached to 'goodness' —and its implementation in justice, truth and generosity—

whatever. It is your duty to yourself, or the wisest thing to do, to drug yourself, so that you shall not feel fear or disappointment. And no emotional idea of 'power,' even, must be attached to the highest knowledge. For would not that be erecting knowledge into a possession—a thing you would fear to lose? Love, too, is in this category. If 'goodness' were an emotional thing at all (as is, for instance, evangelical christian 'goodness') it would necessarily entail *suffering*. And the object of the philosopher is to avoid suffering, or the turbulent 'intoxication' of action or feeling, in every sense. It is in these doctrines of Socrates that you find most readily the ascent to him claimed by the Stoics; and you see in its first state their celebrated *apatheia*, or the 'cynicism' of Antisthenes.

You cannot, logically, 'love' or admire, either, if you *fully* understand. The conclusions to which the intellect and nature of Socrates were directed must have been, I think, a complete nirvana.

But the promiscuous, sceptical, feverish atmosphere of post-periclean Athens affected the mode and development of his teaching. Discrimination into a *prakrita* and its opposite could not, for instance, in those social conditions, be entertained; and the underground cults, such as the orphic, were not the same thing as a widely accepted religion, with its machinery of emotional compulsion. Plato's reasons for the dislike he professed for the writing-down of philosophic dogma indicated that popular uncontrolled instruction must have been a *pis aller*. And, in any case, the main proof of this is, that, in the case of Socrates, a popular teaching culminated in political execution.

It is a fundamental example of Socratic 'irony' which has escaped most people, that he should appear in history as essentially a *popular* teacher. Mr Bernard Shaw has put him forward and held him up to admiration as 'the ideal journalist' of his age. Whether Mr Shaw would have claimed or not that this was a super-irony of his own, the fact remains that Socrates, 'always talking about great market-asses, and brass-founders, and leather-cutters, and skin-dressers' (the raw material of his famous 'induction'), as Alcibiades shows him, lends himself to this interpretation.

Yet of 'the real Socrates' we have the exactest description put into the mouth of Alcibiades in the *Symposium*: 'Know that there is not one of you who is aware of the real nature of Socrates; but since I have begun, I will make him plain to you.

You observe how passionately Socrates affects the intimacy of
those who are beautiful, and how ignorant he professes himself
to be; appearances in themselves excessively silenic. This, my
friends, is the external form with which, like one of the sculpted Sileni, he has clothed himself; for if you open him, you
will find within admirable temperance and wisdom. For he
cares not for mere beauty, he despises more than anyone can
imagine all external possessions, whether it be beauty or
wealth, or glory, or any other thing for which the multitude
felicitates the possessor. He esteems these things, and us who
honour them, as nothing, and lives among men, making all
the objects of their admiration the playthings of his irony.'
(*The Symposium*, 2160.)

If this is intended to enlighten us, and it seems that such is
the case, what it says is as follows. Not only were 'the great
market-asses' and 'the brass-founders' merely the rumbling
stock-in-trade of this supreme market-place performer (properties ironically chosen, ironically handled and ironically dis-
played), but also it asserts that his celebrated language of love,
'his passionate affectation of intimacy for those who are
beautiful,' his display of the amorousness of a fashionable
perversity, likewise were *ironical*. What it says, in short, is that
Socrates was pulling the leg of the Greek *exoletus*, whom
he caressed, as much as he was pulling the leg of 'the great
market-asses'—or the greater asses, their attic owners. He
knew his public only too well, and the simpering but certainly
very argumentative epicene young gentlemen of fashion of the
time: and 'the great market-asses' he used only as stalking-
horses. Similarly, was not the language of love the cynical
gilding of the pill? We cannot be surprised that this peculiar
and very rare sense of fun should have brought him at last to
a violent end—or, at least, an abrupt and involuntary one.

'THE LIQUID BROWN DETESTABLE EARTH'

The liquid brown detestable earth
Has the old cage stink, smacks of dearth.
It has the prison smell of rats.
It preserves the odour of lewd cats.

There was once a Mendip chantecleer
That crowed on a big brown bellied bier.
I thought from his epileptic song
That he had discovered some congenial wrong.

Oh the buxom water rat.
Oh the maiden and the fat cat.
Oh the fat uncorsetted girl
Defending her forgotten pearl.

An eternity of this,
Will lead us to no epiphanies.
Let us make up our packet now:
And tie it with a shop jumper's bow.

'THE LIFE OF MEMORY CONCERNED ME NEXT'

The life of memory concerned me next.
The doomsday-book kept by our kind was neglected,
And the names were becoming objects of envy.
Men disfigured the text.
So the great died. No great name remained unvexed.
When I looked up the name of Nimrod I found him dead.
There was nothing where Pericles had once been written:
Where was Aletho, where Dion? They had forgotten Palamed.
Where was Argisilaus in the clamours of machinery?
Lost I found. It was the same with all the rest.
I persevered but found Scipio the place-name for ruin,
The remorse of Timoleon that made history deny him the
     palm of the soldier
But made him a model to rebuke the martial mind, languished
     in a new shadow
Thrown by adverse anonymous legions, bent on forgetting
Any names but aliases of the raceless, the split-men, untaught,
     unsexed.
I saw the mild morning of Solon being blotted
By the new night, affecting the solar reversal,
Or principles of some fatal irreversible eclipse.
All the gentleness of the western awakening was challenged by
     barbarous sects.
I bid farewell to the still ambered cheeks of the colossi of the
     greek horizon,
So mildly wise with such noble proportion and moderation.
Rome was a speck, a star. Our day I knew was completed.
There would soon be not even the haggard stone that Time
     erects.

EXPLANATORY NOTES

In the following notes, 'Cornell' refers to material in the Wyndham Lewis Collection at Cornell University; and 'Buffalo' to material in The Poetry Collection of the Lockwood Memorial Library, State University of New York at Buffalo. *Letters* refers to *The Letters of Wyndham Lewis*, ed. W. K. Rose (Methuen, 1963).

GRIGNOLLES
Title: 'the name is fabulous', L wrote to Augustus John in 1910 (*Letters*, p. 45.).

ONE-WAY SONG
The following catalogue description was written by L at the request of F. V. Morley, who supervised publication (T. S. Eliot was in the United States).

This considerable poem of two thousand lines is in fact a series of four pieces. *The Song of the Militant Romance* is a lyrical statement of the Romantic attitude in art. There is no counterbalancing statement of the Classical attitude. But in the body of the long succeeding piece, *If So the Man You Are*, a number of Boileau-like verses (and again here and there in *One-Way Song* itself) effect, without comment, the necessary contrast. In *If So the Man You Are* it is mainly in the portion given up to the apology and denunciation put into the mouth of 'The Enemy' (who comes on the stage to carry on for a while the argument) that these Boileau-like couplets are to be found.

Throughout this chain of poems the expression is dramatic: that is to say it is invariably a person, or a variety of persons, speaking. From time to time the personality of the Bailiff of the *Childermass* thrusts its way into the foreground of the dramatis personae and tinctures strongly the character of the verse.

On the whole *One-Way Song*, as this group of poems is named, would probably come under the head of 'satiric verse': and to give an idea of the general nature of the performance, it would be said that, making allowance for the difference in scale, and in the style of art, these verses proceed from the same impulse as that which produced *The Apes of God*, or *The Wild Body*, and in part the *Childermass*. In manner, dramatization and technical intention, it belongs to that group of works.

The Bailiff in L's novel *The Childermass* (1928) rules the after-world with all the techniques of control L believed were used in European democracies. He uses his charm and 'bursting conceit' to manipulate a crowd of appellants wishing to proceed to 'Heaven'. The schoolmaster of 'Engine Fight-Talk' is a Bailiff-figure (see 'Envoi'); note his method of linked emotional and cultural control.

Lewis supplied the following notes on the writing of *One-Way Song* (1) and on verse satire (2) to Kenneth Allott for inclusion in *The Penguin Book of Contemporary Verse* (1950), as a preface to extracts from the poem:

(1) Many people have enquired how it was that I, novelist, pamphleteer, sociologist and so on, suddenly took it into my head to produce a volume of verse. The answer is very simple: I was in the first place, and for years, when young, a writer of verse. One fine day I took it into my head to write a novel. So the enquiry, if at all, should be framed the other way round. Also, however, I was a painter—one strangely 'advanced' for 1913; also I lived in Great Britain. It follows that I found it necessary to become a pamphleteer to defend my paintings against attack and a critic that I might expound the doctrines responsible for the difficulties that so bewildered and angered the public. Then I was a soldier and understood war undoubtedly better than men who had not been that and years afterwards wrote pamphlet-books against new wars (but there are always new wars!). Many other things: books upon 'Time' and upon how men can best manage their rulers. But one fine day I did think I would again express myself in verse. Hence *One-Way Song*.

(2) Verse-satire, in which class *One-Way Song*, I imagine, would be found, belongs to the comic muse. It is far more at home in France than in this country, where Satire must always remain a scandal, and verse be regarded as an occasion for something 'rather lovely', rather than something hideously true, or blisteringly witty. Certainly Mr Eliot in the 'twenties was responsible for a great vogue for verse-satire. An ideal formula of ironic, gently 'satiric', self-expression was provided by that master for the undergraduate underworld, tired and thirsty for poetic fame in a small way. The results of Mr Eliot are not Mr Eliot himself: but satire with him has been the painted smile of the clown. Habits of expression ensuing from that mannerism are, as a fact, remote from the central function of satire.

In its essence the purpose of satire—whether verse or prose—is aggression. (When whimsical, sentimental, or 'poetic', it is a sort of bastard humour.) Satire has a great big glaring target. If successful, it blasts a great big hole in the centre. Directness there must be and singleness of aim: it is all aim, all trajectory. In that sense *One-Way Song* would only be found to answer the description 'satiric verse' in certain sections. In those sections it is, I believe, at least authentic satire.   (pp. 60-61)

Engine Fight-Talk

From L's notes for a reading given at Harvard University in 1940:

This is (if you like) a dramatization of a schoolmaster. The *subject* is his soliloquy about his pupils. His attitude to his class is full of violence and contempt. (Mr I. A. Richards said to me once that the Bailiff in the *Childermass* was a perfect model of how a schoolmaster, or professor, should behave.) This is dialogue—or soliloquy.—If you ask 'What is it all about?' it is the schoolmaster explaining to you (with much bragging) how marvellously he handles his class. This means has been taken (by listening to the Bailiff) of expounding the *historical-romantic* (much of Eliot, Joyce etc).   (Cornell)

L. denied satirizing Auden, Spender and Day Lewis in the first part. In the second part (from 'But poetry came out first') he opposes Ezra Pound's 'exploitation of the very picturesque local-colour of the *past*', and Pound's concept of the past existing simultaneously with the present (*Letters*, pp. 214-5). This is consistent with the first chapter of Book I ('Some Meanings of Romance') and the ninth chapter of *Time and Western Man* (1927). The humiliated Percy Burke puts L's point of view.

p. 22 l. 10: 'Of all the dark 'Medicines' of those peoples under a god' refers to D. H. Lawrence's late work and to *Mornings in Mexico* (1927), attacked by L in *Paleface* (1929).

l. 15: 'What comes out of our Backs': 'It is indeed impossible to point to any one of the many "revolutionary" movements of today that are not conscious returns to former, more primitive, conditions of society' (*Time and Western Man*, Book I, chapter 8).

p. 24, l. 5—p. 25, l. 14: 'I should like to know . . . the light of common day?' This difficult section may perhaps be interpreted in the light of L's general view that the satirist should use contemporaneous materials; Peacock, for example, should not have returned to the sixth century to satirize his own times. Alternatively, L may mean that 'Shakespeare caught the silhouette of Caesar' because he regarded him as a contemporary, and Browne succeeded with 'the Past' in the same way; whereas Robert Browning is a bore in any case. The schoolmaster is an unreliable narrator, however, making the best case he can, and he is eager to bring Shakespeare and the rest to support his argument for the continued contemporary relevance of the past, the 'reversion/To the sweetmeats of the ages', which he approves but which L regards as a soporific preventing critical thought. But the schoolmaster may have a sound point with Ezra Pound's *Cathay* (1915): how is it that the usually 'time-bound Ezra' should have written translations in which the light was so sharp?

p. 25 l. 2: An edition of Sir Thomas Browne's *Urne Buriall* (1658), illustrated by L's private enemy Paul Nash, was published in 1932.

l. 4: 'Why Taliesin steps in Peacock': L objects to Thomas Love Peacock's use of the sixth century Welsh bard Taliesin, and Queen Gwenyvar, in the political satire *The Misfortunes of Elphin* (1829).

l. 8: 'John Keats': perhaps a form of *sortes Vergilianae*, telling the future from passages in Virgil chosen without looking; the Bible and Psalter were also used. Not identified in Keats's life, but unlikely to appeal to L.

l. 9: 'Beckford': *The Travel Diaries of William Beckford of Fonthill* (2 volumes) were published in 1928 and included 'Sketches of Spain and Portugal'. Eleven separate editions of works by Beckford were published between 1922 and 1931.

p. 25   ll. 15-16: 'volume . . . In Portuguese': either the Beckford, or
Elizabeth Barrett Browning's *Sonnets from the Portuguese* (1850), which
were not translations.

The Song of the Militant Romance

Originally entitled 'The *Duc de Joyeux* Sings', a punning reference to
Joyce, who is clearly represented in the drawing of the same title; the
correct name is Duc de Joyeuse. Despite 'Romance' in the title, this
section presents a Lewisian persona approving the non-classical outlook,
and defending the aggression and disturbance to consecutive thought and
to syntax required by true satire. Lewis did not reject all 'romantic'
attitudes: see 'Envoi'.

p. 29   l. 17: 'Guest': *A History of English Rhythms* by Edwin Guest
(1838, ed. Skeat, 1882). He describes 'the "short measures" of John
Skelton.

l. 18: 'my bold Fourteener': George Chapman defends his use of
the fourteen syllable line in his *Iliads*, in 'To the Understander' prefacing
Achilles Shield.

p. 31   l. 25: 'Cleave to the abstract of this blossoming': L's critical
method was to look for the content of ideas and social implication in
fiction, poetry and art; he is urging the reader to approach his own work
in the same way.

If So the Man You Are

Originally entitled 'Song of the Fronts'. From L's notes for the Harvard
reading: 'Written 32 or 33, *If So the Man You Are* is at once a sort of cere-
monial interment of *The Enemy*, and a glorification of that personnage
[*sic*]. The first opening [i.e. Cantos i-xii] . . . is the 'New Enemy' repudi-
ating the legend that the fierceness of the author's *fantoche* [puppet]
had conjured up'. L was concerned to stress that 'The Enemy' was a
persona, not the real Lewis; nor is the voice of Cantos i-xii and xxxi-
xxxiv L himself, but the 'New Enemy'.

p. 37   l. 1: 'I'm no He-man you know': reviewing *The Art of Being
Ruled*, Edgell Rickword remarked that L's thought 'might be tempered
to an even keener edge by some slight admixture with the ecstatic or
"feminine" principle which he keeps at arm's length' (*Calendar of
Modern Letters*, July, 1926); and Rickword's character in 'Twittingpan'
(1931) says: 'Don't you think Wyndham Lewis too divine?/That brute
male strength in every line!'

ll. 9-11: 'Tempyo . . . Monk Ganjin . . . Mitsuda': references to
Japanese Buddhist culture. Tempyo was a period (AD 729-749) known
for the arts, particularly sculpture. 'Han or T'ang': Chinese dynasties
known for a flowering of literature and the arts. L had considerable
oriental interests.

l. 14: 'McClure': mid-nineteenth-century arctic explorer.

p. 37 l. 37: 'I drink, I belch, I stink': 1933 and 1960 editions read 'I belch, I bawl, I drink', but all MSS have the version printed here. Geoffrey Grigson records that L told him T. S. Eliot had asked for the change; if so, it was Eliot's only intervention in the publication of the book. The change was certainly made late, in the (missing) page proofs.

p. 38 l. 21:' "I am the man to shun Hamlet's soliloquy"—questions, heart-ache, natural shocks, calamity of life, all that puzzles the will, and coward-making conscience. The art of pathos, or the artists of it, have their place; but if the artists of pride—like Hawthorne's Ethan Brand (who is Herman Melville)—may end in the white ashes of the lime-kiln, how necessary they are, how much the more so in a general confusion and liquefaction!' (Geoffrey Grigson, *A Master of Our Time: A Study of Wyndham Lewis*, 1951).

p. 39 l. 7: 'shikar': Urdu; shooting animals for sport. 'Bela Kun': Hungarian Communist leader.

l. 12: 'mild-horned coptic ram': in early Christian symbolism the ram signified force, an encouragement to 'fight manfully' in times of persecution. L suggests that he is courageous rather than aggressive in his criticism and satire.

l. 26: 'Chapman': George Chapman (1559-1634), playwright and poet, much admired by L.

l. 27: 'Humbert Wolfe': poet and civil servant, Wolfe (1886-1940) showed 'an urgent belief in goodness and beauty' (D.N.B.) in his verse.

l. 29: 'Churchill': Charles Churchill (1731-1764), satiric poet and radical supporter of Wilkes.

l. 32: 'Cleveland': John Cleveland (1613-1658), satirist and Royalist. With Churchill, one of L's poetic models.

l. 33: 'Isaac Watts': 'liberal' Calvinist and hymn writer, Watts (1674-1748) wrote 'Our God, our help in ages past', etc.

pp. 41-2, Cantos ix, x and xi: Bellerophon's hunt for the Chimaera is here made to take place in the Arctic (canto ix) and by sea (canto x). Canto xi may still be aboard ship, or in the desert. Bellerophon was sent to hunt the Chimaera by the King of Lycia. Homer says of his body, 'heaven . . . put a beauty on/Exceeding lovely' (trans. Chapman, *Iliad* vi), hence 'sun-myth', 'Leonine-headed'. Canto xi: the Chimaera was female, lion at the front, goat in the middle and dragon at the rear. It may stand for the 'feminine' elements in western culture, opposed by L.

p. 46 l. 12: 'Balata': rubber-substitute from gum of South American bully tree.

p. 47 l. 19: 'it swam the Nordic Sea': *Hitler und sein Werk in englischer Beleuchtung* was published by R. Hobbing of Berlin in 1932. L says it was pulped when Hitler came to power in 1933.

ll. 17-20 and 29-30 were omitted from the 1960 reprint of the book, as were lines in canto xxv. That edition was set up from L's own copy, supplied by Mrs Lewis to J. Alan White of Methuen. Mrs Lewis wrote to him: 'You will see the things that Wyndham omitted when he read it at Harvard' in 1940 (23 June 1957). J. Alan White remarked upon the lines struck out very heavily in places, noted that each referred to Hitler or to the Nazis, and decided to excise them (3 November 1958). These deletions were first identified and commented upon by Tom Kinninmont in 'A Note on One-Way Song' in *Lewisletter* 3 (September 1975). T. S. Eliot was obviously unaware they had been made when he wrote in his 1960 'Foreword', 'the text here is identical with that of the 1933 edition'.

l. 22: 'Montalk': Geoffrey Wladislas Vaile Potocki de Montalk, pseudonym of Geoffry Montalk, a New Zealander of Polish descent (b. 1903); poet, printer, translator, editor of *Right Review*, he claimed to be King of Poland. He was tried at the Old Bailey in February 1932 for attempting to publish obscene poetry. Edgell Rickword appeared for the defence (of the principle rather than the person). An appeal fund received contributions from Aldous Huxley, J. B. Priestley, H. G. Wells, T. S. Eliot and others. Asked at the trial if he had anything to say before sentence, Montalk said he wished to go to Buckingham Palace for six months. He was promptly sent to prison for the same length of time.

ll. 25-6: '*Snooty Baronet* . . . is not sold yet': this novel, a satire on the behaviourism of J. B. Watson, and on the literary world, was published in 1932. L may mean that sales were limited by the refusal of Boots' library to stock it.

p. 48. Canto xix: L visited Berlin briefly in November 1930. Five weekly articles resulted, published in *Time and Tide* from 17 January to 14 February 1931. They were revised and expanded as *Hitler* (April 1931). Hurriedly and badly written, both articles and book lack reliable information.

l. 7-8: 'I gave but an impression/Of the Berlin scene, in very impartial fashion': replying to criticism of his articles by Frederick Voigt, Berlin correspondent of the *Manchester Guardian*, L wrote: 'I have, of course, stressed the purely Nazi standpoint. It is essential to do that if one is to secure for them a fair hearing in England, where there are too many Mr Voigts and too few impartial observers' (7 February). L represented Voigt as a Communist partisan for pointing out the brutal prison sentences given to Communists, in contrast to the Nazis, and failed to reply to Voigt's specific points. L had written: 'Whereas the Communist is invariably armed, the Nazi has only had his fists or sticks to defend himself. . . . Yet in spite of the strict orders to the contrary, it does sometimes happen that Nazis arm themselves, in response to extreme provocation, and in face of the certainty of death if they are not in a position to defend themselves' ('Hitlerism—Man and Doctrine: Berlin im Licht!' 24 January). L failed to recognize the facts about Hitler because he was attempting to understand him in terms of his own political theories, developed in the 1920s. Within a few years he regretted his lighthearted approach to German political realities.

p. 48 l. 12: *Germany Puts the Clock Back* (1933) by American journalist Edgar Ansel Mowrer argued that the defeat of the Weimar Republic (1919-1933) led Germany to 'revert to type', to 'Prussianism'—aristocratic and bureaucratic rule. The Social Democrats should have used their years in power to prevent the return of the pre-First World War rulers, but had failed to do so. Mowrer was expelled from Germany, and his book was very widely read after 1937 when revised as a Penguin Special.

pp. 49-50; Canto xx: this was deleted after discussion with F. V. Morley. In June 1933 L had written to Morley, before completing the poem: 'When it is done I think we should meet for an hour or so to consider a few points in it—nothing of importance, only *one* point really'. Presumably this canto was discussed, because Morley wrote on 11 July: 'I would suggest deleting Canto xix [i.e. xx] entire, but leaving the numbering as it is—that is, skip from eighteen to twenty to show that there is a canto missing'. On 26 September L wrote to Richard de la Mare, who was in charge of production at Faber: 'I am sending you a telegram, which I

suggest you print (line block) on the page where the canto is missing'. There was therefore no actual urgency about the telegram; it was rather a question of design.

p. 50 l. 1: 'The house of Kippenberg': Insel-Verlag of Leipzig, taken over in 1905 by Anton Kippenberg, and known for high standards of production and content.

l. 31: 'Linati': Carlo Linati wrote of L in *Scrittori anglo americani d'oggi* (1932): 'Wyndham Lewis non è scrittore populare, è piuttosto un *outcast*, una specie di poeta maledetto che fa parte a sé e che pochi buoni stimano, appunto anche per questo'.

p. 52 l. 16: 'man-of-the-world': the man who knows 'how the world works', and adjusts his thinking to its workings, as opposed to the artist and true critic, who deny the necessity or naturalness of what exists. 'The Man of the World' was a proposed joint title for *The Art of Being Ruled* and *Time and Western Man*. His opposite is the artist's Not-Self: see 'Enemy of the Stars'.

p. 53   l. 11: 'Baerleins, Baums and Goldings': Richard Baerlein, Vicki Baum, Louis Golding, all popular novelists.

l. 33: 'The Business of the Sun!' Here, as often in George Chapman's poetry, what is intellectually and spiritually valuable is associated with the sun.

l. 35: 'Borrow's pets': probably a reference to the gypsies patronized by George Borrow (1803-1881), who took a systematic ('passport occupation') interest in their lives and language.

p. 54   l. 13: 'Insel-Verlag': 1933 and 1960 editions have 'Neusel Verlag'; the MS reading is restored here. 'Neusel' was substituted when Canto xx was dropped—it contained the first reference to the publisher. See note to Canto xx.

ll. 16-18: 'What swastika . . . milch-cow': these lines were omitted from the 1960 edition. See note to Canto xviii.

l. 24: 'D. B. Wyndham's jests': L sometimes received puzzled letters from readers of his books who thought they had been written by D. B. Wyndham Lewis, the Roman Catholic apologist and historical novelist.

p. 56   ll. 10-11: 'Ukiyo . . . Floating World': either Ukiyo-e, 'pictures of the floating world', paintings and prints of the Japanese Edo period, seventeenth and eighteenth centuries (Hokusai and Hiroshige among the practitioners); or *Ukiyo monogatari* (c. 1661), 'Tales of the Floating World', a novel. 'Floating' refers to the evanescent nature of pleasure in this world.

p. 58   l. 25: 'Earp': T. W. (Tommy) Earp (1892-1958), art historian and art critic, was a friend of L's.

ll. 24-25: 'Roy Campbell': (1902-1957) another of L's friends. His first book of poems was *The Flaming Terrapin* (1924).

l. 26: 'Moore, the sturgeon': T. Sturge Moore (1870-1944), poet and dramatist, was a lifelong friend and correspondent whose opinion L valued; he lived in Well Walk, N.W. 3, at this time.

l. 30: 'Read': Herbert Read (1893-1968), who published novels and stories about the First World War as late as 1930.

p. 59   l. 1: 'Richard Aldington': (1892-1962) imagist poet and novelist, made many translations from the Greek.

l. 14: 'Rōnin': wandering dispossessed Japanese samurai warriors; violent, anti-western, pro-Imperial.

p. 60   l. 3: 'Heldenleben': German, heroes'-life. L's first draft read: 'He's the one that may pen/An epic to defend the *Heldenleben*'.

p. 63   ll. 1-3: From L's notes for the Harvard reading: 'Be it marked there is no *Fuhrer prinzip* in the last 3 lines: *Leaders* is a very different thing to *Leader*. And in no possible avatar could the author of *The Art of Being Ruled*—be it marked, *ruled*, not ruling—have trafficked with *Fuhrers*—or *Fuhrers* trafficked with him'.

One-Way Song
From L's notes for the Harvard reading:
That the British Satirist on occasion can forget himself, and refer to what he has done, or is about to do, as 'a poem', I will . . . show you. [In] the two opening pages of 'One Way Song' proper, inadvertently the 'New Enemy', as I have called him, refers to his facetious lucubrations as 'poetry'.
And opposite Canto iv:
But we have gone far enough. The inadvertency of the New Enemy has been sufficiently exposed. This is not *Poetry*, whatever else it is. It is satiric verse. It belongs to the same class as Molière, Ben Jonson, Churchill or Butler. But then so does practically all contemporary verse:—although certainly a good deal of it is much more *romantic*.

p. 67   ll. 3-8: 'Backs of Letters': see Swift's 'Dr Swift to Mr Pope, While he was writing the Dunciad'. 'Now Backs of Letters, though design'd/For those who more will need 'em,/Are fill'd with Hints, and interlin'd,/Himself can hardly read 'em.//Each Atom by some other struck,/All Turns and Motions tries;/Till in a Lump together stuck,/Behold a *Poem* rise!' (1727).

p. 68   l. 9: 'DORSUM': Latin; back.

l. 34: 'Kruschensalted': refers to a contemporary advertisement for Kruschen Salts; they gave you 'that Kruschen feeling'.

p. 70   ll. 19-20: 'pectus est quod facit . . . theologum': 'It is the heart that makes the theologian'; 'pectus' also means 'breast', hence 'Your Front'.

p. 74   l. 17: 'Balistraria': opening in castle walls through which arbalests (crossbows) were fired.

p. 75   l. 9: 'Sketched by Montsurry in the first of the *Bussy's*: *Bussy D'Ambois* by George Chapman (1607). Montsurry says: 'The too huge bias of the world hath sway'd/Her back part upwards, and with that she braves/This hemisphere, that long her mouth hath mocked;/The gravity of her religious face . . . /Turns to th'antipodes; and all the forms/That her illusions have imprest in her,/Have eaten through her back; and now all see,/How she is riveted with hypocrisy' (Mermaid edition, V, i).

p. 76   l. 5: 'From Mab's queenier proto-Britannia, right back to Boadicea': L originally wrote 'From Victoria, through Britannia, right back to Boadicea'. F. V. Morley, after discussion with L, suggested a change because of 'the possible lèse majesté of Victoria'. See next note.

p. 77   l. 19: 'While seven-figure barons guard the throne': L originally wrote 'How golfing princes vulgarize the throne', but this also was considered likely to be troublesome, and was changed.

l. 23: 'Upper Ten': part of the sixth form at Eton College.

p. 80   l. 38: 'on account of *t*': see note to Cantos xxv and xxvi below.

p. 81   l. 7: 'That strange America of mere "events"': *Time and Western Man* presents arguments for the common-sense view of the existence of objects, as against the view deriving from Relativity theory, in which objects come to possess 'a certain timelessness' (Book II, Part iii, Chapter 4). L quotes C. D. Broad: 'Whenever a penny looks to me elliptical, what really happens is that I am aware of an object which is, in fact, elliptical'. L prefers to understand objects as existing commonsensically in time and space, and not subject to perceptual changes; that is, he is committed to the simple sequentiality of time, to the 'chronologic "real" ' of contemporary events.

p. 81   l. 35: 'But that's *not* what's meant': i. e. Bergson, Samuel Alexander, Spengler and the other 'time-philosophers' had no regard for the past as past, but made time the substance of an a-historical reality.

pp. 82-84; Cantos xxv and xxvi: these difficult 'Relativity Cantos' have been explicated by Paul Edwards and Steve Walker, 'Lewis's Critique of Relativity in One-Way Song', in *Lewisletter* 3 (September 1975). Extracts from this article follow.

'For the time-man, then, *t* might in fact be *d*', the argument opens. Time and space are to an extent inter-changeable in the relativist universe. This universe must be regarded as a collection of 'events' (cf. 'that strange America of mere "events" '). A point's existence is itself a sequence of events. To one observer, two events might appear to occur in the same place, and to be separated by three seconds in time. But this is not the only way the events can be regarded. To another observer, moving relative to the first, the events will be separate not only in time, but will be seen to occur at different points in space. It is a common experience among train-users to believe that the train in which one is sitting is moving when the train next to one starts. A quick glance at the platform proves the train to be 'in fact' stationary. No such 'platforms' exist in space, however, so an observer's viewpoint will depend upon his velocity relative to the object viewed, rather than to an ideal fixed point or platform in space. Thus we can say of the observers of the 'event' mentioned above that the first is moving at the same velocity as the object producing the events observed, and the second at a different velocity. A third observer, whose viewpoint is equally valid, moving again at a different velocity, may see the same events as occurring simultaneously, but in different places. So we can say that two events can be considered as separated by an interval of either space or time, depending on your viewpoint; '*t* might in fact be *d*.'

Lewis then goes on to describe, with some irony, the diagram by which these events are represented. This is the 'four-dimensional quartette' (l. 7) which uses Minkowski's conception of time as a fourth 'dimension' alongside the three dimensions of space. What used to be thought of as the motion of matter is represented on this diagram as a collection of events. You are invited to think of these events as existing in normal space where, in order that four dimensions may be imagined, one of the space dimensions is thought of as time. 'Make it a good non-concrete sort of a fit', Lewis says, since it is impossible to visualize; time is not a dimension along which one can move at will as one can in space.

Lewis now appears to go off at a tangent, but the vulgarized philosophy that follows (nicely cleaving to the announced intention 'to charm while I inform') is related to the previous lines, and contains a critique of the notion that time can be considered as an independent line on a diagram against which the changes in things can be measured. The argument derives from a controversy between Gottfried Leibniz and Samuel Clarke. According to Leibniz, we get the idea of time from observing changes in things, and therefore cannot divorce time from those things.

Leibniz is opposing the notion of 'absolute' time, and Lewis agrees with him: 'I stand for no such absolutes.' There is one 'absolute' that he will not abandon, however, and that is God; in which he again follows Leibniz. Leibniz's monads, the simple essences from which his universe is constructed, are, in Lewis's phrase, 'locked . . . up in narrow cells'. They are 'windowless', and not in communication with each other, but with God. In section 8 of the chapter 'The Subject conceived as King of the Psychological World', in *Time and Western Man*, Lewis argues against the idea that the monads should be 'toned down' and given windows through which they could communicate with each other. The purpose of this insistence on the original model can be seen with the help of a quotation from A. N. Whitehead:

> I am toning down Leibniz's monads into the unified events in space or time. In some ways, there is a greater analogy with Spinoza's modes. . . . In the analogy with Spinoza, his one substance is for me the one underlying activity of realization, individualizing in an interlocked plurality of modes.

For Whitehead the monads become, in the metaphor Lewis uses in the lines we are discussing, merely different legs of one giant centipede (or myriapod) which is the 'one substance' of the universe, and travels along on its interlocked plurality of modes. This pantheistic unified view of the universe, expressed in Spinoza's *natura naturans*, Lewis everywhere opposes, arguing in favour of the supreme importance and priority of multiplicity over unity. This is a major theme of the chapter 'God is Reality' in *Time and Western Man*.

In Canto xxvi, Lewis turns again explicitly to Relativity. The opening lines refer to the Michelson-Morley experiments of 1881. These were designed to determine whether 'the Ether' (in the classical sense) existed. The Ether was supposed to be the medium in which light is transmitted, and hence would provide a reference velocity for any moving object; it would be a 'platform' in space. If the Ether existed, it would be possible, as the earth moved through it, to detect variations in the speed of light, as it travelled with, or against the 'etherwind', Lewis refers to 'infra-red' timespaces in allusion to the frequency (and hence colour) shift which would occur if light actually did travel in the Ether. By means of a

'clockwork labyrinth of glass' Michelson and Morley proved that the
Ether does not exist, and that the speed of light will be seen by any
observer, 'stationary' or 'moving', as constant, and always the same
(186,000 miles per second).

Lewis suggests that another 'constant' might be discoverable: 'It's my
belief the Master-Clock does hold/The death-warrant of the four-faced
time-manifold'. The Master-Clock could be considered to be the 'clock'
embodied in Leibniz's monads, synchronized by God. If this 'clock' were
accessible, it would prove (as Lewis believes) the 'death-warrant' of
Relativity, since it would be something against which all other clocks
could be measured. Unfortunately, the monads have no windows, and
nobody has been able to get inside one to check the time. Lewis's argument here is not very useful.

The eleven lines beginning 'Geometry of postulates pretends' (9-20)
returns to the attack on time made in the previous canto. 'Geometry
of postulates' is Relativity theory. Its adepts construct various 'mind
experiments' in which crucial parts are played by travelling clocks. The
argument is clearer if the lines are taken out of their consecutive order
and we start with: 'The infinitesimal interval ds/Is their Achilles heel
and that I bless'. This infinitesimal interval is the limit of the separation
of the two events as they approach each other (the smallest gap between
the two points on the graph) in space and time. This interval is only
definable in terms of a space-time continuum because if space-time has
a discontinuity, a 'jump', then the two objects cannot approach each
other to within an infinitesimal separation at this point. According to
the notion of time held by Leibniz and expounded in the previous
canto, one would expect time to be discrete, not continuous. The same
is true of space ('along with the metre-stick'): 'The infinite divisibility
of space implies that of time, as is evident from the nature of motion. If
the latter, therefore, be impossible, the former must equally be so' (David
Hume, *A Treatise of Human Nature*, Harmondsworth, 1969, p. 80).

Lewis offers the ticking of a clock as an example of a series, between
each of which we cannot know what happens. However close together
the ticks may be there may still be a discontinuity in the interval
between them. This throws the whole theory of Relativity into doubt.
Some modern relativists are now trying to explore the consequences of
this 'discrete' time. It is unlikely that they would be able to do this
without altering Relativity theory beyond recognition. Lewis is correct,
therefore, in identifying 'the infinitesimal interval ds' as an Achilles
heel. With this argument he has snatched 'from beneath it all/That gimcrack apparatus', the clock.

The reference to Mach's principle completes Lewis's case. Mach's
principle, in its original formulation, is 'The comportment of terrestrial
bodies with respect to the Earth is reducible to the comportment of the
Earth with respect to remote Heavenly bodies' (from Ernst Mach, *The*

Science of Mechanics). In a relativistic vocabulary this becomes, 'The local nature of space (space-time) is determined by the distribution of *matter* in the universe.' As in Leibniz's theory, space and time can be seen as 'parasites' on matter. As we have seen, relativists assume a continuity of space-time between, and largely independent of, events.

p. 84   ll. 21-22: 'And your "will",/Why that's wiped out entirely': L valued human will, as creative: 'As a *Will*, and as it manifests itself in us, it certainly seems to be a Will to something pleasant; and in the case of some people to something quite sublime'. He objected to the Behaviourism of J. B. Watson because it attempted to deprive man of active mind or psychic life, describing him as a machine with only instincts and habits (*Time and Western Man*, 'The Subject Conceived as King of the Psychological World', sections 9 and 13).

p. 86   ll. 1-2: ' "Emergent" or "Creative" Evolution . . . /"red" revolution': citing the philosopher Bernard Bosanquet as saying that Time-philosophy 'is the assertion of the immediate and the practical, of the democratic, element, it might be said, in thought', L asks, 'how far Bosanquet was right in identifying these attitudes in philosophy with specific revolutionary idealism, how far the philosophical concept "Time" . . . is in reality the old political "Progress" transformed for the occasion'; but, as here, it remains an unproved (and unlikely) suggestion, demanding that 'democratic' equal 'revolutionary'. Henri Bergson wrote *Creative Evolution* (1907).

p. 86   l. 4: 'Upon the social plane': ' "Time" Upon the Social Plane and in Philosophy' is the chapter of *Time and Western Man* from which quotations in the previous note are taken. L argues that these philosophical theories shape novelists' and academics' views of the actual world.

l. 9: Shelley's poem beginning, 'O World! O life! O time/On whose last steps I climb'.

ll. 21-22: 'See Britain First!' etc.: headlines from contemporary newspaper articles; S. P. B. Mais, *See Britain First*, 4th printing 1933.

p. 87   l. 21: 'Rapa Nui': original name of Easter Island; but it has neither submerged nor emerged for 10,000 years.

l. 33: 'kanaka': South Sea islander.

p. 88   l. 1: 'Chapultepec Park': leisure area on the edge of Mexico City. Chapultepec Castle (now a museum), with its formal gardens, attempts to resemble Versailles, but was built in the nineteenth century.

p. 89   l. 8: 'Klieg-eye': Klieg lights were high-intensity lights, used on film sets. The implication is that Time has been in films, on stage, or 'in the spotlight'.

Envoi

p. 91   l. 10: 'Ridiculous Miss': a play on Horace's 'parturient montes, nascetur ridiculus mus'—'and the mountains laboured and brought forth a ridiculous mouse'.

An earlier draft of the 'Envoi' shows the extent of L's rewriting, and consequent improvements:

The verse is done, the tune is folded up,
Its patent wings. Cut out of ordinary couplets
It's taxied us over the reverse road, back to the start,
Pattern of moths for temporal flight, a rock to a rock,
Up and down, in an empty Pacific.
Hefty singers promising nothing
But a brazen bellows, and giving nothing
But a jazz that mellows, as it goes back
Hoping to find the feathers of its port,
Which is only the chaplet of another atoll.
A desert that was named Elizabeth.

Song Number One was the Bailiff billed in a 'Fight Talk':
That was an overture that needed saying and it was said.
Song Number Two was a sketch of a critical cakewalk—
The romantic standpoint, its programme in prosody, Melpo-
        mene brought to bed.
Song the Third was the electric Me of Boy Number One.
Song the Fourth was the *One-way* lament of the same
Me with which we began.

ENEMY OF THE STARS (1914)

Advertisement: Illustrated from *Blast*.

'Arghol': Hugh Kenner suggests that Arghol is named after the double star Algol, or Alpha Persei (*Wyndham Lewis*, 1954, p. 23). But why should the enemy of the stars be named after a star, or stars? The play's setting, on the borders of Europe and Asia, the characters' 'broad faces where Europe grows Arctic', the reference to Pamir in central Asia, suggest the appropriateness of an Asian name. According to *OED* 'argol' (the spelling occurs in L's typescript) is either the tartar deposited inside casks of fermented wines, and the source of cream of tartar; or dried cow dung used as fuel in Tartary. These unexalted substances, associated with Tartary in Asia, are a possible source for the name.

p. 99 l. 29: 'stress': from typescript; original reads 'street'.

p. 102 l. 20: 'like tired compositor': from Ivan Turgenev's story 'A Correspondence', Letter viii. 'The man himself . . . never attains self-recognition, try as he will; his eyes cannot see his own defects, just as the compositor's wearied eyes cannot see the slips he makes' (*The Diary of a Superfluous Man Etc.*, translated by Constance Garnett, 1899; 1913 edition, p. 294). This story also influenced L's 'Imaginary Letters' of 1917-18.

p. 106 l. 16: 'Well served': typescript reads, rather more clearly, 'he is well served'.

l. 20: 'a grotesque degradation, and "souillure" of the . . . soul':

typescript reads 'a mad degradation and sullying of the . . . soul'.

l. 24: 'Anything but yourself is dirt', etc: This does not mean that other people are invariably held in contempt; it refers back to 'souillure', the inevitable dirtying of the self or ego by unavoidable social and intellectual contact, which is 'other'. The original solitude of the soul never has the opportunity to persist.

p. 112 l. 21: 'Stirner': Max Stirner was the author of *Der Einzige und Sein Eigentum* (1845), translated in 1907 as *The Ego and His Own*. He argues that in order to exist fully the ego must come into possession of all that exists, absorbing it. Swamped by the socialist thought around the 1848 revolutions, it was translated during the turn-of-the-century revival of interest in anarchist thought, which L shared. The ideas of ego and self in *Enemy of the Stars* refer to this book, and when L writes in *Blast* 2, 'There is Yourself: and there is the Exterior World, that fat mass you browse on. You knead it into an amorphous imitation of yourself inside yourself', he is adapting Stirner to the creative process. L misquotes the title ('Einige und Sein Eigenkeit'), which suggests that he had read the German original some years before.

THE IDEAL GIANT

p. 124 Title: the Crowd or Many; violence joins Miss Godd to it.

l. 40: 'salsifis': salsify was far more widely eaten early in the century than it is today.

p. 133 l. 27: 'Golyadkin's double': 'The Double' by Dostoyevsky (translated by Constance Garnett, 1917) concerns Golyadkin's meeting with his double, and his resulting madness. L was much concerned with doubles and dualities (see note to Mani below), and wrote a story entitled 'The Doppelganger' (1954).

p. 134 l. 26: 'We are the civilization for which you are fighting': usually (but wrongly) attributed to Ronald Firbank.

ENEMY OF THE STARS (1932)

This version of the play was revised on a copy of the printed text of the 1914 *Blast* version. A page of this text is reproduced in Omar S. Pound and Philip Grover, *Wyndham Lewis: A Descriptive Bibliography*, 1978, pp. 32-33. The original is at Buffalo. A 'Note' by L reads:

This version of *Enemy of the Stars* differs in detail from that to be found in *Blast No. 1*. There were several versions—the author has restored passages removed from, or not used in, the *Blast* version, and has added new ones. In other respects it is substantially the same.

Lewis wrote the following blurb:

It has been said that this play, the first of its kind in English, influenced the form to some extent of the famous play in the middle of *Ulysses*. The explosive technique employed, together with the economy of statement, is certainly suggestive of the novel form of the stage directions in the Walpurgis Nacht fantasia of Mr Joyce. It is obvious that there are other factors in the *Ulysses* play beside that provided by the form of *The Enemy of the Stars*, but the fundamental structure of the two is noticeably similar. Therefore this play of Mr Wyndham Lewis's, written and published in 1914, marks, in English letters, together with his novel *Tarr* (pub. 1918), the opening of an epoch. Compared with the more fully developed and more technically resourceful work of the master-craftsman author of *Ulysses*, this 'granite flower' might be said to stand as an archaic exemplar of this now fully exploited art form. While his is the most fertile mind of its age, Mr Wyndham Lewis the controversialist has to some extent side-tracked his public and caused them to lose sight of the fact that the controversialist is merely the surface manifestation of what essentially is a fundamental artistic principle. To take a concrete example, the case of Cézanne may be cited. Mr Lewis may very well come to be regarded in literature as an initiator in literary forms in the way that Cézanne was an initiator, in contrast to the more common type of craftsman-exploiter.

The main differences between this and the 1914 version of the play are the introduction of the Not-Self, and the style of the dialogue. The Not-Self ('without others—the Not-Self—there would be no self') originated in 1925, with the essay 'The Physics of the Not-Self', originally entitled 'The Physics of Unselfishness'. The Not-Self is not only others, but others—and all the forces which animate the external world—internalized for the purpose of assessment and criticism. It is a capacity for internalization, contemplation and re-expression particularly the artist's; a self within the artist's self that is detached but active: hence the head-within-a-head illustration to *Enemy of the Stars*. The Not-Self is critical, disintegrative, altruistic and therefore arouses suspicion. In *Literature and Dogma* (1873) Matthew Arnold speaks of the power 'not ourselves', the power of God's righteousness first revealed to the Jewish people, and which passed 'through them to the world'; this is an activity of the internalized and re-expressed Not-Self. Cf. also the Buddha's *anatman* or no-self.

The prose style of the play, especially the dialogue, is a development of the language of L's *Apes of God* (1930), where anticipated commas are frequently omitted. Hotshepsot and Sfox are new characters, and the star imagery is intensified.

Illustration, 'The Play': cf. illustration prefacing *From Magic to Science* (1928) by Charles Singer, showing a 'Vision of the Fall of the Angels' by the mystic Hildegard of Bingen (1098-1197), from her *Scivias*. L possessed a copy of Singer's book; his stars appear to derive from Hildegard's.

p. 147 l. 25: 'Enceladus': Greek mythology; one of the hundred-armed giants.

p. 152 l. 30: 'spunk': on 12 June 1932 Desmond Harmsworth, who had just read proofs of the play, wrote: 'I am pained, as a publisher, by the words "bugger", "arse-face" and "shit"! I very much doubt if they can get by in an edition that is not privately subscribed—in fact, I am confident that they can't. Will you agree to that amount of castration?' (Cornell). L agreed, writing on 15 June: ' "knock the spunk out of him" will be less objected to by *the trade* than the more generally used expression'—which had been 'shit' (*Letters*, p. 210).

p. 158 l. 37: 'Jack of the Cross . . . a dago': St John of the Cross was a Spaniard. He wrote *The Dark Night*, on God's purification of the soul.

p. 160 l. 40: 'Arcturus': among the five brightest stars; situated near the tail of the Great Bear.

p. 161 l. 14: 'Ashtarte': goddess of fertility and reproduction, here transformed.

p. 170 l. 33: 'the seven rishis': the seven stars of the Great Bear.

p. 172 l. 16: 'Shaman . . . Siberians': *The Art of Being Ruled* discusses Waldemar Bogoras's study of shamanism among the Chukchee Eskimos (edited by F. Boas, 1907). The shamans, priests and carriers of spirit-messages, participate in both sexes and are shy and un-masculine.

p. 181 l. 10: 'Rosa Bonheur': French artist (1806-1856), painted animals ('The Horse Fair') and landscapes, with great attention to detail.

l. 31: 'Stirner': L again gives wrongly the title of Stirner's book, as 'Einige und Sein Eigenkeit'; see note above. 'The master of Marx' is Hegel; Stirner belonged to the group of left Hegelians that included Strauss, Feuerbach and Engels.

p. 183 l. 11: 'Weinstube': German, small wine bar.

l. 38: 'Mensur': German students' duel.

p. 186 l. 4: 'Tarquin': Sextus Tarquinius raped Lucretia.

l. 33: 'great rolled-up rotter': L originally wrote 'bugger'; see note above.

p. 188 l. 18: 'bum-face': L originally wrote 'arse-face'; see note above. L wrote to Harmsworth: '*Arse-face* becomes *bum-face*—in the American sense of "silly" '.

PHYSICS OF THE NOT-SELF

This essay is an attempt to find a non-ethical basis for the definition of 'goodness', by equating it with knowledge, and identifying Socrates' 'knowledge' with the Buddhist Nirvana. The first sections of the essay, down to 'The Husbandry of "Goodness" ', defend, often with extreme irony, the importance of the intellect, while recognizing the contempt in which it is usually held.

p. 200 l. 7: 'John Burnet': author of *Early Greek Philosophy* (1892 and many editions).

l. 40: 'upanishadic Karma': the upanishads were Hindu philosophical treatises, elaborations of the Vedas. Concerned with the nature of reality, they are radically monist (cf. L's dualism). Also concerned with the nature of knowledge and the types of valid knowledge, which are L's interests here. *Karma* is the doctrine of the happy or unhappy rebirth of the soul according to *karma* (works) in the previous life. The soul could be reborn as an animal.

p. 201 l. 9: 'avidya': Sanskrit; ignorance of the Buddha's Four Noble Truths, which once known allow the soul to transcend ephemeral reality.

l. 13: 'Yâ jñaval Kya' (or Yàjñavalkya): semi-legendary Indian sage and teacher who originated the doctrine of *karma*.

p. 202 l. 5: 'the atman': the self: the anatman is the no-self.

l. 7: 'Mani': founder of the Manichaean church and religion in third century Persia. His dualistic theory opposed Light (absolute good) and Darkness (radical evil).

p. 204 l. 5: 'Sileni': participants in Dionysiac rituals, hence the contrast with 'temperance and wisdom'.

THE LIFE OF MEMORY CONCERNED ME NEXT

A fragment based on a reading of Plutarch, particularly *Solon and Publicola, Dion and Brutus, Timoleon and Aemilius Paulus*. Apparently a persona is speaking; L would not say 'Men disfigured the text' in his own voice. The interest in memory, machinery, 'split-men' and the opposition to militarism are characteristic of L's thought and terminology in the 1920s.

p. 206 l. 12: 'The remorse of Timoleon': Timoleon saved the life of his brother in battle, but when the brother turned tyrant, was present at his assassination. His grief was so great 'that almost twenty years passed without his setting his hand to a single conspicuous or public enterprise' (vii). Plutarch comments: 'For repentance makes even the noble action base' (vi).

TEXTUAL AND BIBLIOGRAPHICAL NOTES

In the following notes the annotation 'Pound-Grover' refers to entries in
Wyndham Lewis: A Descriptive Bibliography, by Omar S. Pound and
Philip Grover (Dawson, 1978), in which the present volume appears as
A-50.

GRIGNOLLES (BRITTANY)

First published in *The Tramp: An Open-Air Magazine*, II, 3 (December
1910), 246 (Pound-Grover E-8). The text of the present edition is that
of a holograph fair copy (Cornell), which differs from the printed version
in omitting initial line capitals and in other details of punctuation, which
have been reproduced here.

ONE-WAY SONG

First published by Faber and Faber Limited on 2 November 1933, probably in an edition of 1500 copies. There was a signed and limited edition of forty copies (Pound-Grover A-20a and A-20b).

Under the title *Song of the Fronts* the poem is first referred to in a
letter to the publisher Desmond Harmsworth in June 1932. Later Cassell
took up an option, and under the same title it was released, for £50
returned advance, to Faber in June or July 1933, by which time it bore
its present title. Faber released *One-Way Song* to Mrs Lewis on 6 June
1957.

The impetus for the 1960 edition came from Ezra Pound, who proposed
shortly after L's death in March 1957 that a number of works might be
republished. J. Alan White of Methuen and T. S. Eliot at Faber and
Faber had some difficulty in understanding all Pound's proposals, but his
clearest suggestion emerged as the most practicable. White and Eliot
made their decision on 11 June 1957. Eliot promised first a paragraph
for the dust-jacket, and later a Foreword. This was delivered on 5 August
1959, when the book had been in proof since May of that year.

It was published by Methuen on 25 February 1960, in an edition of
1500 copies, and less than 100 copies were remaindered on 27 July 1972
(Pound-Grover A-20c). T. S. Eliot's Foreword included the whole of the
publisher's note, or blurb, from the first edition, which was written by L.
This edition was set in type from a copy used by L for a reading given at
Harvard University in 1940, and passages deleted from that copy do not
appear in the Methuen edition. See notes to 'If So the Man You Are',
Cantos xviii and xxv. The facsimile of a telegram, which replaced Canto
xx of 'If So the Man You Are' in the 1933 edition, was deleted, and the
cantos following renumbered.

The Penguin Book of Contemporary Verse, edited by Kenneth Allott
(1950) reprints the following: 'If So the Man You Are', Canto xiv;
'One-Way Song', Canto xxiv (Pound-Grover D-10).

Artscanada 114 (November 1967) distributed a recording, made at Harvard in 1940, of L reading 'If So the Man You Are', Cantos xvi, xvii and xxxi; and Cantos i-iv of 'The Song of the Militant Romance' (Pound-Grover J-8). This recording was reissued as 'Wyndham Lewis reading extracts from *One-Way Song*', *Audio Arts* I, 2 (1974).

The text of the present edition is based on the 1933 edition, collated with the holograph and typescript (top copy) at Buffalo. Canto xx of 'If So the Man You Are' is from this source, and is printed here for the first time. Corrections have been introduced from L's Harvard reading copy; from corrections made by L in a copy inscribed to Will Rothenstein (both at Cornell); and from a list of corrections proposed to L by Faber in 1933, approved by him, but not introduced into the 1933 text (Faber archive).

ENEMY OF THE STARS (1914)
First published in *Blast* 1 (1914), 51-85 (Pound-Grover C-1a).
Reprinted in Wyndham Lewis, *A Soldier of Humor and Selected Writings*, edited by Raymond Rosenthal (New English Library, Signet Classic), 1966, pp. 74-105 (Pound-Grover A-44).

The present edition reprints the *Blast* text, with the preliminaries and parts I-II corrected against the typescript (top copy) of a slightly earlier but substantially similar draft (Cornell). The *Blast* errata have been incorporated, and obvious typographical errors corrected throughout.

THE IDEAL GIANT
First published in *The Ideal Giant, The Code of a Herdsman, Cantelman's Spring-Mate* (privately printed, London Office of *The Little Review*), 1917 (Pound-Grover A-1).
Reprinted in *The Little Review* VI, 1 (correctly: V, 1), May 1918, 1-18 (Pound-Grover E-55).
Reprinted in *A Soldier of Humor* (1966), pp. 113-129. (Reprints from *The Little Review*).

The present edition reprints the first publication. Four lines of dialogue are lost from the first American publication, and consequently from the second.

ENEMY OF THE STARS (1932)
First published by Desmond Harmsworth Limited on 1 July 1932 (Pound-Grover A-17).
The present edition reprints the 1932 text, with minor corrections.

PHYSICS OF THE NOT-SELF
An earlier version was published in *The Chapbook* 40 (1925), 68-77 (Pound-Grover E-89).
The present text is that of the 1932 edition.

'THE LIQUID BROWN DETESTABLE EARTH'

Previously unpublished. From a holograph MS at Buffalo. The handwriting suggests a date in the early or mid-1920s.

'THE LIFE OF MEMORY CONCERNED ME NEXT'

Previously unpublished. From a holograph MS at Cornell. The handwriting suggests a date in the late 1920s.

A number of further fragments of poems held at Buffalo are not thought to be worth publishing.

BIBLIOGRAPHY

In 1934 L remarked 'On the whole my press for *One-Way Song* has been better than for any book of mine' (with the exception of his book on Shakespeare). The following bibliography is selective, with an emphasis on reviews, which are selectively annotated.

GENERAL
C. H. Sisson, *English Poetry 1900-1950: An Assessment*, 1971.

ENEMY OF THE STARS
Stella Benson, *Time and Tide* 23 July 1932, 819-820.

Douglas Garman, *Scrutiny* December 1932, 279-282.
   'The "Not-Self" is a shadowy enough concept to put forward as the representative of human value'.

Alan Munton, 'Desmond Harmsworth, Lewis's Publisher', *Lewisletter* 8 (August 1978), 3-7.
   Describes the confused circumstances of writing and publication of the 1932 version.

ONE-WAY SONG
Geoffrey Grigson, *Morning Post* 10 November 1933, 15.
   'Its concise form, as though it had been carved out of a larger mass of words, is the chief sign of its poetic excellence. The parts seem to me related almost inevitably. Mr Lewis has integrated his vigorous imagery and vigorous content, and he has controlled his couplets and fourteeners with a major dramatic artistry. He drives into a single line what a poet of normal ability would leave lying about in a dozen.
   'If his sense of persecution reminds one unhappily of Swift, we are reminded of Swift also by a kindred excellence. Swift, Dryden, Pope, John Oldham, and Churchill—all, I believe, would readily shake Mr Lewis by the hand'.

Herbert Palmer, *New Britain* 29 November 1933, 51.
   'For the most part a satire of the new, soulless verse of this machine-age'. L denied this in a letter of 13 December, and expanded the denial in articles of 3 and 10 January 1934.

G. W. Stonier, *New Statesman* 2 December 1933, 710, 712.
   'Chat and rhetoric, a rhythm like a wheezy pump and lines of unexpected beauty'.

Gilbert Armitage, *New Verse* February 1934, 12-17.
   ' "A plague o' both your houses" is his reply as artist . . . to capitalist Capulets and communist Montagues alike'. In 'If So the Man You Are' 'the affinity with Dryden is manifest. The unforced, natural diction, the

large virile utterance, are both there'. 'One is reminded of one of Dryden's latest direct descendants, Byron—particularly in "One-Way Song" itself'. A comparison 'reveals a frivolity in Byron . . . with which the flippancy of Lewis is quite untinged'. 'Lewis is generally a better versifier than Byron'. 'The "snooty tit-for-tat", in sections xxvii and xxviii of "If So the Man You Are", recalls the temper and tempo of Donne's fourth satire, directed against the court'.

Times Literary Supplement 15 March 1934, 185.
'It is difficult at times to apprehend clearly the intellectual attitudes underlying the various themes'.

James Bramwell, *London Mercury* 29 March 1934, 459-460.
'A distinguished and independent mind, not limited by political convictions or personal dislikes, but relentless in exposing all types of bogusness'.

Hugh Gordon Porteus, *Criterion* April 1934, 492-494.
'An uncommon sense of responsibility and concern for human destiny'.

James Neugass, *New Republic* 12 August 1934, 53-54.

Walter Allen, *New Statesman* 2 April 1960, 496.
'Stands in relation to his prose works much as *Pansies* do to Lawrence's novels and essays: it states a familiar position in a fresh way'. 'As a piece of writing it could scarcely be more uneven'.

John Wain, *Spectator* 4 March 1960, 327-328.
'I am repelled by it, as I am by all Lewis's writings'.

Robert Armstrong, *Poetry Review* July-September 1960, 172-173.
'I must confess that I am repelled'.

T. S. Eliot, 'Foreword' to 1960 edition, 7-10.
'It would be only the very obtuse who would dismiss the verse as *doggerel*'.

Graham Hough, *Listener* 21 April 1960, 720, 722.
'Doggerel'. 'A wealth of ideas, enormous fertility of illustration, verbal adroitness, gusts of energy'.